MATCHED TO THE
QCF

Sarah Pilbeam

Edited by: Maureen Eve...

CUSTOMER SERVICE

NVQ Level 2

HODDER
EDUCATION
AN HACHETTE UK COMPANY

146134

146134 BUS

Orders: please contact Bookpoint Ltd, 130 Milton Park, Abingdon, Oxon OX14 4SB. Telephone: (44) 01235 827720. Fax: (44) 01235 400454. Lines are open from 9.00 to 5.00, Monday to Saturday, with a 24-hour message answering service. You can also order through our website www.hoddereducation.co.uk

If you have any comments to make about this, or any of our other titles, please send them to educationenquiries@hodder.co.uk

British Library Cataloguing in Publication Data
A catalogue record for this title is available from the British Library

ISBN: 978 1 4444 15743 7

This Edition Published 2012
Impression number   10 9 8 7 6 5 4 3 2 1
Year   2016, 2015, 2014, 2013, 2012

Hachette UK's policy is to use papers that are natural, renewable and recyclable products and made from wood grown in sustainable forests. The logging and manufacturing processes are expected to conform to the environmental regulations of the country of origin.

Cover photo © Neustockimages/iStockphoto.com.
Illustrations by Peter Lubach.
Typeset by Pantek Media, Maidstone, Kent.
Printed in Italy for Hodder Education, an Hachette UK Company, 338 Euston Road, London NW1 3BH.

Contents

INTRODUCTION

This guide has been designed as a resource to help you understand and complete the Level 2 NVQ Certificate in Customer Service.

The Level 2 NVQ Certificate in Customer Service is suitable for those dealing with internal or external customers in any organisation. The qualification will enable you to recognise and acknowledge the skills, knowledge and understanding required to deal with customers and to provide excellent customer service.

There are four themes within the Level 2 NVQ Certificate in Customer Service:

1. Impression and image

2. Delivery

3. Handling problems

4. Development and improvement.

This book will cover a number of units from the qualification and at least one from each theme. The units addressed are as follows:

- Mandatory units – Unit F1, Unit F2
- Impression and image – Unit A4, Unit A10, Unit A11
- Delivery – Unit B2
- Handling problems – Unit C1
- Development and improvement – Unit D1, Unit D3.

The qualification is presented in units and within each unit there are learning outcomes (LO). Each LO is broken down into a number of assessment criteria (AC). (Note: For information about unit certification and credit values contact your awarding organisation.) The assessment criteria address both performance and knowledge. In this qualification all knowledge criteria are addressed in the final learning outcome of the unit.

Features of the guide

Throughout each chapter there are learning features that will help you build the knowledge and then the evidence you need to gather for each unit. The features are:

- **Unit learning outcomes** for each unit, published by the standard setting body and used across all awarding organisations (AO).
- **Assessment criteria** for each learning outcome, published by the standard setting body and used across all AOs.

- **Tutorials** providing information to help you understand the learning outcomes and assessment criteria for that unit, and to provide some background information for customer service as a topic.

- **Case studies** with questions, consisting of scenarios to stimulate your thought processes about customer service situations. There is no requirement to record your answers to the questions in writing unless instructed by your tutor or assessor.

- **Reflective activities** with questions to help you think about customer service situations that you have experienced. There is no requirement to record your answers to the questions unless instructed by your tutor or assessor. However, your reflections might provide you with prompts and reminders later when you are gathering evidence to prove your competence.

- **Performance evidence activities** with questions and prompts to get you thinking about your customer service role and the context in which you provide products and services. The outcomes of these activities are a useful tool for collecting evidence of your performance. It might be helpful to record your answers in writing or to voice record your responses in preparation for meetings with your tutor or assessor.

- A **summary** – each chapter concludes with some suggestions to help you pull your thoughts and evidence together for the unit and the assessment methods that your assessor might use to help you demonstrate your competence against the national standards.

- A **learner evaluation** asking you to reflect on your learning from completing the unit guide. Again, this does not have to be recorded in writing although it could be very useful to record the answers to use in reviews with your line manager, supervisor, assessor or tutor, or possibly in a job interview. Documenting your learning throughout your working life is an effective way of showing that you use experience to influence your performance and behaviours.

- **Examples of evidence** have been provided for each unit at the end of the book and will give you some ideas of how to meet some of the national standards.

Using the guide

The two mandatory units (Unit F1 and Unit F2) have been covered in depth but not all optional units have been addressed. However, all units follow a similar theme and language so as you progress you will become familiar with the terms and requirements of the units and this will help you to understand what you need to do to cover the knowledge and performance for each optional unit.

Each chapter can be used as a step-by-step guide for a unit or as a reference book to help you to interpret key terms and phrases used in the customer service profession.

At the end of the book you will find some examples of evidence to support each unit covered in the guide. Note that these are snapshots and do not cover all criteria in the unit.

A glossary of terms used in the chapters is also provided at the end of the book to help you understand the language of the qualification and customer service terms.

Working with an assessor

Each section is intended to help you to develop towards being a more 'thinking' and 'reflective' customer service professional. Your qualification centre will allocate an assessor who will work with you to identify the customer service tasks you can already do in your present role (or have done in a past role) and those you could do in a future role. You may also have a tutor to guide you while you are building your knowledge (often the tutor will be your assessor as well). Once you have the knowledge and are fully competent your assessor will look at your evidence and make a judgement of your customer service skills and knowledge against the national standards. Over time you will build a portfolio that will demonstrate this competence.

The virtual advisor

The guides have been written as if you have a 'virtual advisor' sitting beside you in the absence of your assessor or tutor, interpreting the knowledge requirements, providing you with support, reminding you what the standards are asking of you and to help you refresh and test your knowledge and understanding.

Involving other team members

You will need to involve your line manager, team leader or supervisor from the beginning of the Level 2 NVQ Certificate in Customer Service. They will be able to provide development opportunities, alongside your assessor, and support and review your progress in a way that will help you to successfully complete each unit and contribute towards the overall performance of the organisation. They will also be able to contribute to confirming your competence in customer service with your assessor.

Presenting your evidence

You and your assessor will need to agree the most appropriate way of presenting your evidence, but here are some suggestions:

- An electronic portfolio: you could upload your evidence to e-portfolio software or simply store the evidence in electronic format on your PC and back up on a memory stick or a CD.
- A paper-based portfolio: you could build a folder with hard copies of your evidence.
- A combination of both: a paper-based portfolio with paper evidence record sheets and assessment documents; supported by audio records of professional discussions, question and answer sessions, witness interviews and some product evidence stored on a CD or memory stick.

Types of evidence

The evidence that you present should cover as many of the performance criteria as possible and cross-reference to other units, so you will need to discuss this with your assessor at the beginning of the qualification. Your assessor will make an assessment judgement on the suitability of the evidence that you present and will have the final say as to what is acceptable.

Some examples of acceptable evidence are given below.

- Observation: Your evidence could be an observation by your assessor of you working and interacting with your customers and colleagues.
- Professional discussion: This is an effective way to capture your evidence for performance and knowledge. The discussion (which can be captured as an audio recording) should be carefully planned in advance with your assessor and there must be a written record of the outcome produced by your assessor.
- Questioning: A written or verbal record of your assessor asking questions to test your knowledge, to clarify situations, or build on evidence already collected.
- Personal statement or reflective account based on the activities in the unit. This should be supported by other evidence, such as work products or witness testimony.
- Case study: an account of a customer incident, transaction or problem. You should provide the date, time of day, type of customer and explanation of the transaction, problem or incident and the outcome. This should be supported by other evidence, such as work products or witness testimony.
- A discussion to identify previous experience or achievement. This is referred to as Recognised Prior Learning (RPL).

All of the above can be supported by:

- Work products: copies of work produced by you that demonstrate your competence over time. For example, your personal development plan, work documents. You do not need to print out the work products and put them in your portfolio as your assessor can look at them in the workplace and document that they have been seen.
- Witness testimony from your line manager, others in the organisation or customers, confirming your competence. This testimony can be in writing or recorded as an audio interview by your assessor.

It is a good idea to include a range of evidence from different sources. You can be as innovative with your evidence as your organisation, assessor and resources will allow, so if permitted you could use video, photographic or audio recorded evidence.

In some cases you will not be able to include work product evidence because of confidentiality or data protection regulations. In this instance you can ask your manager or a colleague to confirm that you have participated in customer service transactions, discussions and/or meetings and that you are able to recognise typical customers and their expectations. To save time, this can be verbal confirmation to your assessor, or it can be in written format on headed paper, a witness form provided by your assessor or via email. There should also be confirmation that you follow the organisation's procedures for customer service. Alternatively, your job description, performance review or development plan might support your performance in your role.

Other qualifications

Some of the chapters in this book may contribute towards some of the knowledge aspects of the following units in the Level 2 Certificate in Principles of Customer Service (Technical Certificate).

The units in the certificate are:

1. Understand the principles of customer service – Chapter 1 (Unit F1) , Chapter 2 (Unit F2), Chapter 3 (Unit A4)
2. Understand the rules of customer service – Chapter 2 (Unit F2)
3. Understand the use of communication in customer service – Chapter 3 (Unit A4), Chapter 4 (Unit A10) , Chapter 5 (Unit A11)

Picture credits

Every effort has been made to trace the copyright holders of material reproduced here. The author and publishers would like to thank the following for permission to reproduce copyright illustrations:

Figure F1.3 © pressmaster – Fotolia
Figure F2.3 © imageegami – Fotolia
Figure A4.2 © Cultura Creative/Alamy
Figure A10.4 © Image Source/Corbis
Figure A11.2 © diego cervo – Fotolia
Figure B2.2 © Ingram Publishing Limited
Figure C1.3 © Monkey Business – Fotolia
Figure D1.4 © Kenishirotie – Fotolia.

COMMUNICATING USING CUSTOMER SERVICE LANGUAGE

Learning outcomes

Learning outcomes for Unit F1:
1. Identify customers and their characteristics and expectations
2. Identify their organisation's services and products
3. Know how to communicate using customer service language

Introduction

This unit guide is a resource to help you gather the evidence that you require to achieve Unit F1, a mandatory unit in the Level 2 NVQ Certificate in Customer Service. It can be used as a learning resource if you are new to your role, are studying customer service in preparation for work or as a refresher if you are an experienced customer service professional.

Communicating using customer service language – what is Unit F1 about?

Unit F1 is about:

The language and basic principles that are the heart of customer service and the skills needed to communicate effectively with customers and colleagues

Source: Extract from Unit F1 purpose and aim

You will be able to describe how your customer service role fits into the organisation and how you contribute to good customer service. You need to be able to explain the services or products that your organisation offers and how it delivers customer service. All professions and sectors of industry have a specialist language or jargon that external customers and newcomers to the industry find difficult to understand. The customer service profession is no different and there are examples in the tutorials that follow. It is vital that this language is used in the right time and place with the appropriate people. Internal customers and colleagues will often have a higher level of technical and business knowledge and newcomers need to be provided with development opportunities to learn the appropriate language. There may be specialist language that you will never use with some of your customers. It is important you are aware of the language you use in your organisation and in your sector in general.

The following customer service language is widely used in organisations and it is important that you have an understanding of the meanings of these terms:

- **Service offer**: A service offer defines the extent and limits of the customer service that an organisation is offering.
- **Moments of truth**: In any customer service procedure there are several points when customer awareness of the quality of customer service is particularly high. 'Moments of truth' means the points in a transaction, service delivery or customer relationship at which customer expectations are at their sharpest and most demanding.

Source: www.instituteofcustomerservice.com

Figure F1.1

There are many customer service terms that may be used specifically in your organisation. Take some time to consider and understand this terminology so that you can answer some of the questions in activities. See if you can find a definition for the following:

- Service level agreement
- Mission statement
- Customer rights
- Added value

For further information a customer service language glossary can be found at: http://www.instituteofcustomerservice.com/1848/Glossary.html

Completing this unit guide

To complete this unit guide you will need to:

1. Read through the information in each section.
2. Read the case studies and reflective activity and use the questions to help you test your understanding.

There is no set format for working through or recording your answers in these sections, just use them in a way that suits your learning style, unless otherwise instructed by your assessor or tutor. The case studies and reflective activity are linked to the assessment criteria in learning outcome 3, which focuses on the underpinning knowledge and understanding for Unit F1. Learning outcome 3 has been presented first so that you understand the background to the criteria in learning outcomes 1 and 2. If you work through this section first you will find that your performance evidence will be easier to identify and present to your assessor.

Learning outcome 3 – Knowledge evidence

LO3 Know how to communicate using customer service language

- The tutorial section is designed to explain the assessment criteria. In this section your virtual advisor will provide you with information to help you interpret the national standards.
- The case studies and reflective activity will help you to prepare to discuss and explain your understanding of customer service with your assessor.

Learning outcomes 1 and 2 – Performance evidence

LO1 Identify customers and their characteristics and expectations
LO2 Identify their organisation's services and products

In both learning outcomes the performance evidence activities, assisted by your virtual assessor, will help you reflect on your performance and knowledge as a customer service professional. They will also help you to identify and gather evidence.

Why do I need to communicate using customer service language?

Customer service is not just a job – it underpins everything you do in your work role. If you are involved in providing products or services to others, whether they are internal or external to your organisation, it is essential that you are able to:

- recognise your typical customers
- identify your customers' expectations
- discuss expectations with colleagues using recognised customer service language
- follow the organisation's rules and procedures
- communicate with customers using the most appropriate methods
- explain the products and services that you can offer to your customers
- know where to obtain customer service information
- know what to do when problems arise.

The cycle of excellent customer service

It is important to use your skills, knowledge and understanding so that you continuously reflect and evaluate your own and others' customer experiences. The cycle of excellent customer service (Figure F1.2) illustrates four important stages of any customer service transaction.

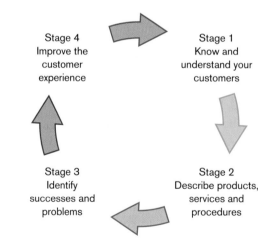

Figure F1.2: The cycle of excellent customer service

Stage 1 Know and understand your customers

This is the vital starting point. You will not be expected to immediately know and understand every individual customer that you provide a service to, but you will need to have a broad knowledge of who your customers are and what their needs and expectations are going to be.

Stage 2 Describe products, services and procedures

As a customer service professional you should know what you are providing to your customers, for example, the features and benefits of the products and services and the way you must deliver these. You also need to be aware of the procedures, rules, regulations or legal guidelines that impact on that provision.

Stage 3 Identify successes and problems

It is essential to reflect both as an individual and with colleagues and customers what has gone well and where there have been problems. This is the stage that will make a difference between you and your competitors, help you to build on your strengths and improve where things are not meeting customer expectations.

Stage 4 Improve the customer experience

This is the stage where you do something about the areas that are not going well and share good practice with colleagues where things are good. Although this is described as stage 4, this process never stops and each stage links with the next. By improving the customer experience you go to the next stage of the cycle again – know and understand your customers – but this time you will know a little more about your individual customers and how you can meet their needs. And so the cycle of excellent customer service continues!

Knowledge evidence for Unit F1 (LO3)

As stated earlier, we will begin with learning outcome 3 (LO3). This contains the knowledge criteria for the unit and it is essential that you have this knowledge to underpin your performance. Note that the criteria in LO3 have been grouped into common themes and follow the cycle of excellent customer service and therefore are not in number sequence. We therefore begin by considering stage 1 of the cycle of excellent customer service – know and understand your customers.

LO3 Know how to communicate using customer service language

Assessment criteria

3.1 Identify the differences between an internal customer and an external customer

3.8 Identify who are their customers

3.9 Describe the main characteristics of typical customers that they deal with

3.3 Describe the connection between customer expectations and customer satisfaction in customer service

3.7 Identify the part they play in delivering customer service

TUTORIAL 1 with your virtual advisor:

Read through this tutorial so that you can meet the requirements of the assessment criteria shown above.

3.1 Identify the differences between an internal customer and an external customer

3.8 Identify who are their customers

It is important that you are able to identify your customers and can recognise who is an internal or external customer.

An internal customer is someone within your organisation with whom you have contact. They could be the person who sits at the desk next to you or they could be in another department, building or location, relying on you to provide them with products, information or services. Your internal customer could be anyone with whom you come into contact on a regular or occasional basis and who is affected by what you do or provide for them. If you order the stationery for the office team then in this context they are your internal customers. If you supply a sales spreadsheet for an accounts administrator on the last day of the month, they are your internal customer.

Your external customer is anyone outside your organisation to whom you supply products or services. For instance, for a customer service professional working in a hospital their customers are people coming in as patients or visitors. When a customer service professional works in a shop it is easy to see who the external customer is: it is the person who walks through the door wanting to purchase an item or needing help or advice about a product. However, the external customer could also be the management team of the shopping centre in which the shop is located. Shopping centres are often owned by a separate organisation and the retailer may have to provide information about their sales figures and pay a percentage of their turnover, as rent, to the managing organisation in return for services like cleaning and maintenance. However, the shopping centre owner is also providing a service to the retailer. This arrangement could also be seen as a service partnership.

Consider the following questions in relation to your customer service situation. Making notes will help you to collect your thoughts and you can use them when you meet with your 'live' assessor or tutor.

Questions

1. What are the differences between an internal and external customer?

2. List your internal and external customers.

3. Can you be more relaxed and familiar with your internal customers?

4. Do you use different language to internal customers, for example, more specialised 'speak' or jargon?

5. If you are dealing with an external customer would they understand such jargon?

6. Do you have different communication methods with internal customers? For example, face-to-face, instant messaging and email, text, telephone?

7. How do you communicate with the external customer? Is it through telephone, email, text, the internet or by letter?

8. Consider these differences and how they can influence the customer service that you provide.

3.9 Describe the main characteristics of a typical customer that you deal with

First you need to reflect on what a characteristic is. In this context it might be the typical age range of your customers, their gender, location and any cultural differences as well as specialist groups. Note that this is not a matter of stereotyping; instead it is about understanding the needs that will be generated by their characteristics and what you and your organisation can offer them. Perhaps your customers will have special requirements, for example they might need to use a lift rather than stairs or they might need extra help to access their goods or services. They could be in a vulnerable state when they make contact with your organisation.

It is important to consider the location of your customers: they may be located remotely or even in an international setting, requiring you to deal with them by email or the internet. This will mean that you cannot see them to read their signals or body language. There may also be language barriers that you have to consider, so you will have to gather information about how you can help to meet their needs, perhaps by speaking through language interpreters. You can also determine your customers' characteristics by collecting feedback through questionnaires or surveys. It is important that you take time to reflect and analyse the outcomes of this feedback in order to meet the needs and expectations of your customers.

3.3 Describe the connection between customer expectations and customer satisfaction in customer service

The primary expectation of most customers is to be treated in a friendly and polite way and to obtain the information, products and services that suit their needs. They may also have expectations that are based on your organisation's service agreements or promises. For example, your customer might be expecting to be assisted within a certain time frame (the telephone will be answered within four rings, or an order to arrive within three working days) and to be given the seamless level of service that your organisation has promised. An example of such a promise is 'this is a one-stop shop: we will deal with your enquiry in a friendly and prompt way so that you do not have to call us again'. Whatever the promise, the experience should match this and once the customer service exchange has been completed the customer should go away happy.

Proactive customer service professionals will carry out research with customers to find out what they want from an organisation and how they feel about the product or service received. How often are you asked to complete a feedback card after a meal or complete a short questionnaire before entering or exiting a website? Amazon and other large web retailers ask you to review the product that you have just purchased. These feedback mechanisms enable the organisation to link expectations to satisfaction. This technique of collecting feedback can be carried out for almost any product or service (internally or externally delivered).

3.7 Identify the part that they play in delivering customer service

This is an area you will need to reflect on and perhaps is the most important of all the criteria in this learning outcome. If you do not understand your role you cannot provide good customer service. Everyone has a part to play in an organisation and your role is important. You can find out exactly what your role is through your induction programme, on-the-job training, your job description, role profile or a performance review with your manager.

If you are not informed about the products and services, the customer service levels, the rules, the procedures and your objectives or targets, then the overall customer experience could be damaged. If customer expectations and satisfaction are affected it will have a negative impact on the whole system, so it is important that you realise how you connect with the people, products, procedures and promises and the importance of your role in determining the satisfaction of all of your customers.

You will need to know who is who in the organisation and what they do. If you do not understand where you fit in then talk to your manager, supervisor or colleagues and find out what happens before and after you have played your part. Keep your knowledge of the products and services up to date from the organisation's website, promotional materials and adverts: there is often a wealth of information available if you take time to look.

The case study provides an opportunity for you to read about a customer service professional and consolidates some of the information from the tutorial. You can use this to reflect on the situation and answer some questions. Again, you do not have to write your answers down unless your tutor or assessor has asked you to do so.

CASE STUDY 1 Ellie and the nursery section

Ellie works in the baby and nursery section of a large department store. The customer promise is: 'we will treat you honestly and provide excellent value and service'. Ellie is a member of a small team, the others being the manager and two experienced part-time staff. She often has to work on her own and today her manager is out at a meeting, one colleague is on holiday and the other member of staff is due in at 10.30. Ellie receives a telephone call at 09.30 from a colleague in another branch. She asks if they have a pushchair in stock; this particular model has been advertised on the website and in the brochure and they have sold out. She checks if Ellie could transfer one to them today as they have a customer who needs it urgently. Ellie checks the stockroom and finds that they have two in the stockroom and one on display. They agree one can be transferred. When she comes off the telephone Ellie realises that she is not sure of the procedure so decides to wait until her manager returns from the meeting.

As soon as her colleague arrives at 10.30 Ellie goes on her break. When she returns they are busy dealing with a delivery.

A woman and her daughter come in and look around and go over to the pushchairs on display. They take their time looking and then approach Ellie to ask her a question: they have a Mini and want to know how the pushchair wheels are removed to get it in the car boot. Ellie is not sure but has a go and manages to get them off so that they can see. After some discussion they go for the model that Ellie had promised to the other branch. Ellie goes into the stockroom to get the pushchair and can only find one! She recalls her earlier telephone conversation and panics. She returns to the women and says that she does not have any in stock. They are very disappointed and leave the store.

Ellie asks her colleague where the other pushchair has gone and she tells her she has sold it. Ellie tells her about the customer who has just been in and her colleague informs her that she could have offered the one on display and she could have let the customer try it in the boot of her car before selling it. Ellie remembers the transfer and her colleague tells her she should have taken it down to 'goods out' before 10.00 as she has missed today's van.

Questions

1. Who are Ellie's internal and external customers?

2. What were Ellie's internal customers' expectations?

3. What were Ellie's external customers' expectations?

4. How satisfied were Ellie's customers today?

5. What impact have the events of today had on her customers and her organisation?

6. What should Ellie have done to meet her customer's needs and expectations?

We now come to the second part of the cycle of excellent customer service – describe products, services and procedures.

LO3 Know how to communicate using customer service language

Assessment criteria

3.2 List their organisation's services or products
3.4 Describe why organisation procedures are important to good customer service
3.5 Explain why teamwork is central to good customer service
3.6 Identify the service offer of their organisation
3.11 Identify who's who and who does what to deliver customer service in their organisation
3.13 Explain how to find information about their organisation's services or products

Read through this tutorial so that you can meet the requirements of the assessment criteria shown above.

3.2 List their organisation's services or products

The previous tutorial highlighted the need to know about the products and services the organisation offers. This information is available to you from a number of sources including your manager/supervisor and colleagues, the training that you had when you started your job, on-going training through team meetings and communication sessions, your customer promise, brochures, advertisements, the internet, your suppliers and manufacturers. To be able to list the services and products you need to be aware not only of the products and services offered within your own department/area/branch/office, but also who supports and complements you and what they can offer. You should be able to identify the features and benefits of each product to your customers.

What is a feature? It is a point that describes what a product or service can do for the customer. Take the example of a mobile telephone. Its features might include the type of telephone and the operating system, size and resolution of the screen, whether it is contract or pay-as-you-go, whether it enables the user to access the internet and has a camera/video, etc.

What is a benefit? Every feature has a potential benefit for a customer, but a benefit to one might not be to another. A benefit of a SMART telephone could be that you can access email and the internet; this might suit a business user but would be completely unnecessary for a customer who carries a telephone around for emergencies and only uses it once in a while.

As a customer service professional you need to look at all your products and services and decide what features and benefits might appeal to your typical customers. This is an activity best undertaken with colleagues so that you can all agree and standardise your approach. Be aware that one size does not fit all!

3.4 Describe why organisation procedures are important to good customer service

In every organisation people are essential to the delivery of the products and services but the procedures are the glue that holds it all together. If procedures are not set up and followed then each person will interpret and deliver the service in a different way. This inconsistency could affect customer satisfaction, or worse, result in legal requirements not being met. An example that everyone can relate to is when a customer has to return faulty goods to a shop or supplier. There are legal requirements that have to be followed in this instance and consumer rights to be considered. If an organisation does not have a sound procedure in place the organisation could be breaking the law and in danger of prosecution. It could also result in the customer making unreasonable demands that they have no right to; this in turn could affect the profitability of the organisation. Organisations will have many procedures in place to cover all stages from ordering to delivery and all are designed to protect the staff/organisation and ensure a consistent and seamless delivery of customer service.

The methods of communication that you and your organisation use are important to good customer service. The internet is fast becoming a way to deliver products and services quickly and efficiently. This method will suit independent customers who are IT literate and do not want to wait on the end of the telephone. However, customers who prefer contact with people might prefer to use the telephone or to visit the service provider and see someone face to face. Email has overtaken the sending of letters but this has resulted in communication becoming shorter and adopting a 'no frills' approach. Text messaging and social media are fast becoming other abbreviated forms of electronic communication, particularly to inform customers of an impending delivery of goods. Some mobile telephones now have a video capability so that you can see the person you are speaking to. With a move from paper to electronic mediums, the customer service professional must ensure that they have the necessary skills and training to keep up with technology and procedures, while retaining the principles of good customer service skills.

3.5 Explain why teamwork is central to good customer service

We looked at how you identify the role you play in delivering customer service in Tutorial 1 earlier in this chapter. However, you cannot deliver customer service alone and will be working with others such as your team leader (manager, supervisor,) team champion, buddy, colleagues, suppliers and sometimes the customer.

Within a team all members have a part to play and will have particular strengths and specialism. They might be the process person who sets procedures, processes and objectives and ensures that targets and service levels are maintained. They might be the auditor who will carry out the monitoring and assessing of the team members. Other team members might be experts on the technical aspects of the job, while others come up with ideas. Good teamwork means ensuring that all team members communicate and interact with the leader and other team members. A good team is equal to the sum of its parts and teamwork enables the more experienced members to support and help the others, but also allows *all* team members to present ideas and play a part in customer service.

3.6 Identify the service offer of the organisation

What is a service offer? A service offer can be anything that lists or states the standards of service that your customers can expect from you. It may also be known as a service level agreement, and is often measured by targets, for example, how many rings before the telephone must be answered, how many calls answered per hour or day. It can also be measured by the promises that your organisation advertises to its customers, such as free delivery on orders over £30.

Many organisations publish an overall statement of intent often known as a Charter, Mission Statement or Promise. The service levels in these documents are usually not so specific and each area, branch or department will have specific targets that they have to meet, depending on their market and customers. An organisation might have a range of service offers tailored to the needs of each customer. In summary it is what the organisation promises to do for its customers, both internal and external.

3.11 Identify who's who and who does what to deliver customer service in the organisation

This is about not just understanding your own role in the organisation but the roles and responsibilities of others, including those in your immediate team (they might be handling different accounts or customers), the people that buy in the products or sell the organisation's services, those that provide after-care and the teams that link or interrelate with your team. The list is endless and will depend on your organisation.

There are many ways you can seek to understand the role of others, including asking questions at team meetings and networking with people from other areas of the organisation. Many people now use social networks to find out about their friends and families and some organisations now operate their own Facebook site. You can also obtain information by looking at the company intranet, attending training sessions or just by speaking to your manager or supervisor.

Be curious! Find out and absorb information because you never know when it will come in useful. You might not know the answer to a customer question but you will know someone who does!

3.13 Explain how to find information about their organisation's services or products

We have just discussed the importance of knowing 'who is who and who does what' in the organisation. Of equal importance is having knowledge of the organisation's products and services. That means not only having an awareness of the products and services within your direct responsibility but also what other products and services are available in other departments, branches, depots or sites. The sources of information are very similar: colleagues, managers, suppliers, briefing sessions, the intranet/internet and just being inquisitive. You may even be a user of some of the products and services yourself, so make sure you do your research and can answer questions from a customer's perspective.

Now read the case study below and answer the questions that follow to consolidate some of the information covered in Tutorial 2. Once again, you do not have to write your answers down unless your tutor or assessor has asked you to do so.

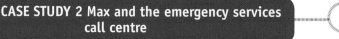 **CASE STUDY 2 Max and the emergency services call centre**

Max works in a call centre for the emergency services. He is part of the front line team, responsible for receiving calls and emails from the public regarding complaints about noise and nuisance, lost property, crime and emergencies. He also makes calls to follow up enquiries and reports. Max also receives internal calls from emergency service personnel. He never knows who will be the next caller or what they will ask or need him to do.

Max has a supervisor and eight experienced colleagues within his team, including a shift trainer and tutor and knowledge experts in legal and regulatory matters. The team work sets of six days on and four days off. The shift times vary from early to late nights and the centre is staffed 24/7. The teams meet at least once every set of shifts to discuss targets, problems and issues and they are provided with information updates.

There is a published customer charter on the internet, promising to provide appropriate help and guidance and a professional and high quality service at all times to all members of the local community. This is highly visible so customers know what to expect.

Max works to service level agreements – both team and individual targets. He and his team also have to meet service offers and agreements set by external organisations like the council and government. The targets have to be met daily. He receives a spreadsheet at the end of each month showing how he has met his targets. He has a job profile and this outlines his role and responsibilities and his objectives are measured in his one-to-one meetings and personal development report.

Max works with a variety of equipment, including a telephone and computer. He must have an awareness of different types of software, including telephone packages and databases tailored for the organisation. He also uses generic word processing, email and spreadsheet software and he has access to the internet and the company intranet.

Max has knowledge of many processes and procedures and as he can often be dealing with life and death situations, he must ensure he uses the documents and processes accurately and effectively. If he does not this could affect many people. When providing information to his customers Max needs to be aware of legal and regulatory requirements relating to human rights, data protection, disability discrimination, health and safety, criminal law and local council regulations. If Max cannot answer a customer's question or query he has to know who to go to or where to look for a solution. Not surprisingly, Max has received intensive training over the period of six months and is not expected to be fully proficient for another six months.

Questions

1. Who are Max's internal and external customers?

2. Name two of the services that Max provides to his customers.

3. Why is it important for Max to know and understand his services and procedures?

4. Who can provide support, advice and information to Max?

5. Why is teamwork important to the customer service Max delivers?

6. What is the call centre's customer service offer and promise?

7. Name others in Max's team who contribute to the delivery of customer service.

8. Identify at least four customer service terms in the case study and explain what they mean.

Look back at stage 3 of the cycle of excellent customer service – identify successes and problems (Figure F1.2). We will now look at how you measure the impact of your customer service on your customer and whether they are satisfied with the outcome.

LO3 Know how to communicate using customer service language

Assessment criteria
3.10 Identify what impresses their customers and what annoys their customers
3.15 Explain how the way they behave affects their customer's service experience

TUTORIAL 3 with your virtual advisor:

Read through this tutorial so that you can meet the requirements of the assessment criteria shown above.

3.10 Identify what impresses their customers and what annoys their customers

We all require products and services – the bus to work, our mobile telephone, insurance, NHS services, the weekly food shopping – the list is endless. Everyone is a customer and you will know from experience what impresses you and what annoys you. When dealing with your customers you need to think about how you would want to be treated if you were in their shoes and how, as a customer service professional, you can impact on the experience. However, it is also important to realise that your values and requirements as a customer will not always match those of all your customers.

The term 'moments of truth' refers to the point in a customer transaction when customer expectations are at their highest, in other words, the 'make or break point'. Consider the example of the customer service professional in a hotel reception who takes your order for a wakeup call. If the call fails to happen, causing you to miss an appointment or even your breakfast, then it will be difficult to retrieve the relationship. But if all runs like clockwork and the wakeup call is successful, the hotel is on its way to delivering excellent customer service, providing the rest of the hotel team do their bit!

In a complex customer service transaction there might be a number of moments of truth, points at which the customers' satisfaction will be met or not. Take a moment to reflect on some of your past or current customer transactions and think about why they went right or wrong.

3.15 Explain how the way they behave affects their customer's service experience

We mentioned earlier the importance of knowing your customer, product, process and promise. As a customer service professional it is vital you are aware of your own behaviour, too. How many times have you been subjected to a negative experience because of the way a person has spoken to you, either face to face or over the telephone? Perhaps you have felt patronised because someone has assumed you do not understand the product, for example when buying a car or a new computer. Maybe you have complained about a product or service not meeting the customer promise and have been treated like a naughty child by the person dealing with your complaint! We have all been through these experiences or been told about them at some time. From a customer's perspective it is how *they* feel after the incident, not how the person dealing with them feels. Therefore, as a customer service professional you need to treat each person you come into contact with as an individual and according to their needs.

Often the way we react to a person or situation can be a reflection of how we feel about ourselves at that moment in time. We need to recognise and understand our own emotional state (known as emotional intelligence) before we can be effective in our work role. As a customer service professional you need to be aware of your trigger points – what annoys you –and make sure that you do not prejudice your customer communications as a result. You need to be aware of what makes you feel good and what makes you feel bad and how to turn bad to good.

You also need to recognise how other people are feeling and this can be done through listening, looking out for signs in tone of voice, language (both verbal and body) and facial expressions, and adjusting your delivery to suit their needs. Consideration needs to be given not only to your behaviour but also to your communication skills of listening, speaking and writing. Using the correct method of communication will also affect your customer's experience and this will be discussed in more depth in Chapter 3, Unit A4.

When your customer (internal or external) enters into a transaction, they have certain expectations. They may have done some research and therefore have an idea of what suits them. In such a case they will then decide where to go to obtain what they want/need and there will be some discussion before they make their final decision. However, if the atmosphere during this discussion is negative because of your emotional state or behaviour then there will be conflict. Ways to combat this are to assess your own emotions, observe or listen to your customers for clues about their emotional state, be pleasant and be aware of the tone in your voice. Remember the primary expectations of your customer are to be treated in a friendly and polite way and to obtain the information, products and services that suit their needs. If you cannot provide the information your customer wants or you do not know the answer, do not make up an answer or make promises you cannot keep, consult with a colleague instead.

The reflective activity below is designed to help you to start thinking about your reactions and feelings when you encounter different customer service scenarios. We are all customers on a regular basis, so this activity is from the perspective of you as the customer. It will help to prepare you to collect evidence that will demonstrate your knowledge, understanding and practical skills in customer service. Write down your reflections if you wish as they may be useful in discussions or sessions with your assessor or in the preparation of evidence.

REFLECTIVE ACTIVITY 1

Think about a scenario when you were the customer and all your needs and expectations were met. Where were you and what did you want? Was it a product that you were buying or a service that you required? What impressed you about the transaction and why?

Now think of a time when you experienced a less than satisfactory situation and you were annoyed by it. Was it the customer service professional that caused the annoyance? Was it a system or procedure or another member of staff that caused the problem?

If you cannot think of any examples then ask a colleague or friend about their experiences.

Questions

1. In the case of the positive experience, how did the behaviour of the customer service professional affect the situation?
2. In the case of the negative experience, what could the customer service professional have done to change the situation?
3. When was your 'moment of truth' in both examples?

We have now reached Stage 4 in the cycle of excellent customer service and this is where you can make a difference to your effectiveness as a customer service professional. This is the evaluation stage of the process when you use feedback and comments from customers to improve the service that you provide.

LO3 Know how to communicate using customer service language

Assessment criteria

3.12 Describe the kinds of information they need to give good customer service to customers
3.14 List typical customer service problems in their work and who should be told about them

TUTORIAL 4 with your virtual advisor:

Read through this tutorial so that you can meet the requirements of the assessment criteria shown above.

3.12 Describe the kinds of information you need to give good customer service to customers

As a customer service professional you must aim to meet your organisation's customer service promise. This might be cascaded to you in the form of objectives and targets and identified in your job description, role profile and personal development plan/review. It may also be conveyed through one-to-one meetings with your manager or during your appraisal.

Although this provides you with a framework with which to operate, you must also be able to identify the information you need to improve and provide even better customer service. This can be achieved in many ways, for example you might collate a guide that you keep on your desk or at the point of sale, with useful leaflets, information bulletins, telephone numbers, contact addresses, products specifications and who to contact about specific subjects. Perhaps you use a manual provided by a manufacturer or supplier. You could have the 'live' product on your desk so that you can talk your customer through their question or query. Many customer service professionals will have access to customer databases and are able to access information from this source.

Other information sources could be team meetings, suppliers visiting the organisation, subject experts delivering awareness sessions and the internet and intranet. The list is endless and will depend on the resources available both inside and outside your organisation.

Another source of information about products and services is direct or indirect customer feedback. Many customers know what they want but just do not know where to access it. The questions and comments that they make can provide you with information about what you need to provide. Feedback can be formal, through questionnaires and surveys, or informal, collected from passing comments. We often do not realise how valuable such passing comments are in helping to improve the service we give. We will explore this in more detail in some of the optional units.

3.14 List typical customer service problems in their work and who should be told about them

It is often said a customer problem is a gift! If we do not know what is going wrong or our customers' concerns with the service they are receiving we cannot do anything about it. A customer service professional should welcome feedback from every source. How many times do you receive a comment from a customer which provides you with a signal that they are not happy? How do you deal with a situation like this? Many customers do not bother to contact you about what has gone wrong but they will happily tell their family and friends who in turn pass it on to more people. In such a case you will be unaware that you have lost a number of potential or actual customers. Stories of what has gone wrong can evolve like Chinese whispers and eventually a simple mistake can be exaggerated into a really large problem. If you pick up on comments like this then you need to gather information and facts and either deal with the issue yourself, or pass it on to someone who can.

Take a few moments to reflect on your organisation's processes for capturing information about customer problems and complaints. If they are well documented procedures then it will be clear who the information needs to go to but if there are no processes in place it might be left to you to decide who should be told about them. A customer will want action to be taken as swiftly as possible but some decisions may be beyond the limits of your responsibility. You may need to discuss with your manager, supervisor and colleagues what can be done by you and what has to be passed on to others in the team.

Look again at the cycle of excellent customer service (Figure F1.2). You need to collect information from your customer and do something about it to improve their customer service experience. The cycle never ends because there is always a problem to solve and changes to be made. Each time you make improvements you are demonstrating that you are increasing your understanding of the needs of your customers, so you come back to stage 1 of the cycle.

We are now going to revisit Ellie in the nursery department and look at how she can develop and take control of her knowledge and understanding. Read through the case study and then answer the questions that follow.

CASE STUDY 3 Ellie and the nursery department re-visited

Ellie has been working in the department store for two months and this is her first job in a retail environment. She went through an induction and was given a buddy to help her settle into the job. Her buddy was from another department and was there for the first week. The buddy introduced her to other people in the branch, where things were located, information about the mission statement, rules and regulations and the general procedures relating to the company discount, staff dress and health and safety and welfare issues.

Ellie's manager is very busy attending meetings and going to conferences. The two part-time members of staff are always busy; they seem to know everything and expect Ellie to pick up information without being directly told. Ellie has to keep asking them about different products and when they are not around she has to muddle through on her own. The other day a customer came in and told Ellie a cot was not fit for purpose and her rights were not being met. Because she is busy Ellie often forgets to tell her team members about these incidents. She keeps hearing her colleagues mention things like features and benefits, POS and exchange policies and she is embarrassed because she does not know what they mean. Ellie was taken to task about the transfer incident and told by her manager that she had to 'buck up her ideas'. She knows that she is not performing effectively and is worried that she will lose her job. She speaks to her buddy and comes up with a wish list:

- Have a better understanding of how to deal with problems and understand who can help her resolve them.
- Obtain more product knowledge.
- Understand the jargon used.
- Gain an understanding of procedures, for example, how to transfer items to another branch.
- Be part of the team.
- Be confident like her colleagues.

Questions

1. Where can Ellie access the product knowledge?
2. Who can she approach to expand her knowledge of the department and store procedures?
3. How can she obtain and retain the little gems of information she hears from the team?
4. Who can help her with the problem-solving issue?
5. How can the manager and team help Ellie?

Performance evidence for Unit F1 (LO1 and LO2)

The case studies and reflective activity so far have given you the opportunity to consider the customer service provided by two characters in different customer service settings and to think about customer expectations from your own experiences.

The next section in this unit is designed to help you focus on the learning outcomes and performance requirement of Unit F01 and prompt you to think about how you can evidence this through your customer service role. It is expected that the evidence that you generate for this unit will also cross-reference with some of the optional units that you have selected. The virtual advisor will guide you to collect the evidence that you need to complete this unit.

Performance evidence is different from knowledge evidence and requires you to identify events that have happened in the course of your job in a real work environment. You will have to prove that the customers really exist and the events or incidents really happened – your assessor will help you to do this. The ways that you can present the evidence will be explained in Tutorial 5 below. You should answer the questions in the context of where you work and your provision of customer service. This time it *is* important for you to record your answers in writing as this will be the foundation of your evidence. However, you need only write notes to remind you where the proof is located.

LO1 Identify customers and their characteristics and expectations

Assessment criteria

1.1 Recognise typical customers and their expectations

1.2 Discuss customer expectations with colleagues using recognised customer service language

1.3 Follow procedures through which they and their colleagues deliver effective customer service

Performance evidence activity 1

Write down or make notes to discuss your answers to these questions:

1. Who are your internal customers? What are their expectations?
2. Who are your external customers? What are their expectations?
3. What do you promise your customers that you will do for them?
4. Provide some examples of both your internal and external customer service offers.
5. How do you store and communicate information to your internal and external customers?
6. List some of the customer service language that you use within your organisation and with colleagues and suppliers.
7. What procedures do you need to follow to maintain customer service levels?
8. How do you work with colleagues to ensure that the service offer is maintained?
9. What responsibilities do they have in their role and who has specialist experience?
10. Where and how do you discuss customer service levels and problems with colleagues and your manager?

TUTORIAL 5 with your virtual advisor:

This tutorial is not intended to take the place of meetings with your assessor but to offer some support and a refresher in his or her absence.

The information that you have collected from Performance evidence activity 1 above will help you to present some evidence for learning outcome 1. In Tutorial 1, assessment criterion 3.9, you were asked to consider the main characteristics of a typical customer that you deal with. Using the notes or thoughts you had for this tutorial, you should be able to gather sufficient evidence to demonstrate that you can recognise what a typical customer wants and expects from you and your organisation and thus meet the requirements of assessment criterion 1.1.

In Tutorial 2 you were asked to list your organisation's service offer. In order to cover assessment criterion 1.2, you will need to present some evidence of meetings (formal or informal or conversations with your colleagues where you have discussed your customers' expectations. This is an activity that your assessor might be able to observe you carrying out or a colleague could confirm that you have taken part in a meeting by providing you with a witness statement.

Finally, you will need to demonstrate that you follow your organisation's procedures to deliver effective customer service. This means complying with the rules and regulations, understanding and using the processes that are in place to help you deliver your products or services to your customers and meeting their individual needs. (Complying with rules and regulations is covered in more detail in Chapter 2 Unit F2, where some of the activities will help you to identify the legal and regulatory requirements that underpin your customer service provision.) Assessment criterion 1.3 can be evidenced through observation, professional discussion or personal statement; your assessor will guide you to the most appropriate method for your situation.

LO2 Identify their organisation's services and products

Assessment criteria
2.1 Outline their organisation's services and products to customers
2.2 Greet customers politely and positively
2.3 List the information they need to deliver effective customer service and where that information can be found

Performance evidence activity 2

You should write down your answers to these questions so that you create a record.

1. What products and/or services do you provide to internal and external customers?
2. Select two products or services and highlight their features and benefits.
3. What are your priorities and targets in delivering customer service?
4. How do you know that you are meeting your priorities and targets?
5. How do you obtain product and service information?
6. How do you keep up to date with changes in your products and services to meet your customer's needs?

The next two activities will help you to pull all of your preparation together and show your evidence through some 'live' examples of customer service transactions. Your answers to these activities can be used in final evidence but will need to be endorsed or supported by witnesses or work products.

Performance evidence activity 3

Reflect on two customer service transactions when you had a successful outcome, one with an external customer and one with an internal customer. Incorporate as many of the points and details highlighted in your answers to Performance activities 1 and 2.

- When and what were the 'moments of truth'?

Remember to make notes of your thoughts.

Performance evidence activity 4

Reflect on two customer service transactions when something went wrong, one with an external customer and one with an internal customer. Incorporate as many of the points highlighted in Performance activities 1 and 2.

- When and what were the 'moments of truth'?
- What could you have done to have changed the outcome?
- How will you ensure that customer service is improved in future?

Again, remember to make notes of your thoughts.

TUTORIAL 6 with your virtual advisor:

This tutorial is not intended to take the place of meetings with your assessor but to offer some support and a refresher in his or her absence.

The information that you have prepared and collected from Performance evidence activity 2 and the examples you have prepared for Performance activities 3 and 4 will help you to present some evidence for LO2.

The assessment criteria above are best covered through observation by your assessor: they can see you working and interacting with your customers and colleagues, the methods of communication that you use and how you inform customers of the products or service. The observation could capture all three of the above assessment criteria.

If this is not possible a professional discussion with your assessor or a personal statement/case study (verbal or written) based on the examples that you have prepared in Performance activities 3 and 4 will enable you to show your assessor what you did and how you documented it. The example should be supported by work products such as emails or letters you have completed for customers, a description of the procedures that you use, customer databases and feedback forms.

Evidence in context:

An example of sample evidence for some of the learning outcomes of Unit F1 has been included at the end of the book.

LEARNER EVALUATION ACTIVITY

The last activity is the learner evaluation. Each section in this chapter is intended to help you to develop yourself towards being a more thinking and reflective customer service professional. The learner evaluation requires you to reflect on your learning from completing this unit guide. Once again, this does not have to be written; however, it could be very useful to record your answers for use in reviews with your line manager, supervisor, assessor or tutor or possibly in a job interview.

Documenting your learning throughout your working life is a very effective way of showing that you use experience to influence your performance and behaviours. Reflect on what you knew at the start of the unit and what you know now.

1. What have you learned from completing this unit?

2. Identify three phrases that were new to you.

3. How will completing this unit affect your customer service within your organisation?

4. Highlight an improvement that you have made as a result of completing this unit.

If you are working towards Unit D3 Develop personal performance through delivering customer service, your evaluations might also provide you with some foundation evidence.

Figure F1.3: Greeting customers politely and positively

Summary

This concludes the unit guidance for Unit F1 Communicating using customer service language.

You should be prepared to submit evidence for both the knowledge and performance aspects of the unit learning outcomes:

LO1: Identify customers and their characteristics and expectations
LO2: Identify their organisation's services and products
LO3: Know how to communicate using customer service language

You will now be able to describe how your customer service role fits in to the organisation and how you contribute to good customer service. You will be able to explain the services or products that your organisation offers and how you are expected to deliver customer service.

It is likely that the knowledge and performance evidence you produce for this unit will cross-reference to the following Customer Service units:

- Unit A4 Give customers a positive impression of yourself and your organisation
- Unit A10 Deal with customers face to face
- Unit A11 Deal with incoming telephone calls from customers
- Unit B2 Deliver reliable customer service
- Unit C1 recognise and deal with customer queries, requests and problems
- Unit D1 Develop customer relationships

Learning outcomes

Learning outcomes for Unit F2:

1. Follow their organisation's customer service practices and procedures
2. Know how to follow the rules to deliver customer service

Introduction

This unit guide is a resource to help you gather the evidence that you require to achieve Unit F2, a mandatory unit in the Level 2 NVQ Certificate in Customer Service. It can be used as a learning resource if you are new to your role, are studying customer service in preparation for work or as a refresher if you are an experienced customer service professional.

Follow the rules to deliver customer service – what is Unit F2 about?

This unit requires you to understand the rules that apply to customer service delivered by your organisation and how they apply to you and your job.

The organisation from which you draw your evidence must be the organisation you work for or the organisation in which you have realistic work experience. It may be the whole of the organisation or the business unit, division or department with which you are involved.

> *Source: Adapted from Unit F2 purpose and aim and evidence requirements*

You will be required to demonstrate how you follow the rules of your organisation to deliver customer service to your internal and external customers. This includes following all relevant procedures and processes, many of which will be underpinned by European and UK laws.

For more information on the customer service terms used in this chapter, go to the customer service language glossary at www.instituteofcustomerservice.com.

Health and Safety information can be accessed at www.hse.gov.uk and information regarding the Equality Act 2010 can be found at www.acas.org.uk.

Completing this unit guide

To complete this unit guide you will need to:

1. Read through the information in each section

2. Look at the case study and reflective activity and use the questions to help you to test your understanding.

There is no set format for working through or recording your answers in these sections, just use them in a way that suits your learning style, unless otherwise instructed by your assessor or tutor. The case study and reflective activity are linked to the assessment criteria in learning outcome 2, which focuses on the underpinning knowledge and understanding for Unit F2. Learning outcome 2 has been presented first so that you understand the background to the criteria in learning outcome 1. If you work through this section first you will find that your performance evidence will be easier to identify and present to your assessor.

Learning outcome 2 – Knowledge evidence

LO2 Know how to follow the rules to deliver customer service

- The tutorial section is designed to explain the assessment criteria. In this section your virtual advisor will provide you with information to help you interpret the national standards.

- The case study and reflective activity will help you to prepare to discuss and explain your understanding of customer service with your assessor.

Learning outcome 1 – Performance evidence

LO1 Follow their organisation's customer service practices and procedures

In addition to the learning outcomes, in this unit there are performance **evidence requirements** that indicate the circumstances or conditions under which you should present the evidence.

You must provide evidence of following the rules to deliver customer service:

- during routine delivery of customer service

- during a busy time in your job

- during a quiet time in your job

- when people, systems or resources have let you down.

The cycle of the rules of customer service

The cycle of the rules of customer service (Figure F2.1) illustrates four important stages of any customer service transaction.

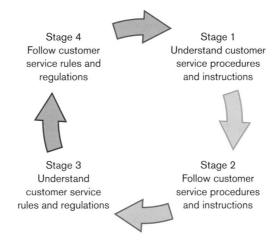

Figure F2.1: The cycle of the rules of customer service

Stage 1 Understand customer service procedures and instructions

The first stage in the cycle relates to learning about and understanding the internal procedures and instructions that apply to your customer service role. When you started your job your organisation should have given you an induction where they informed you of:

● the organisation's products or services

● the expected standards of appearance and behaviour

● your working hours

● the aims, objectives and targets of your area of work and the organisation as a whole.

This information should be updated on a regular basis through meetings, training, one-to-one meetings with your supervisor and networking with colleagues. It is your responsibility to make sure that you understand what is expected of you.

Stage 2 Follow customer service procedures and instructions

Stage 2 of the cycle is about how you apply what you have learned about the products, service and procedures. It is also about demonstrating appropriate behaviour and attitudes, in line with the organisation's ethos, values or charter.

Stage 3 Understand customer service rules and regulations

As an employee (whether voluntary, contract, temporary or permanent) the employing organisation must provide you with information about its rules and the legal requirements that you must follow in your job role. This will normally be carried out at induction and whenever there are changes to the rules or laws. The legal obligations that all customer service professionals must be aware of are health and safety, equality and diversity and data protection. However, there will be other laws, regulations and codes of practice that will be specific to your organisation or sector. It is vital that you are familiar with and fully understand anything that impacts on what you deliver, say or do for your customers.

Stage 4 Follow customer service rules and regulations

The final stage relates to how you apply and follow the laws, rules and regulations in your customer service role, and how you recognise when to go to others in the organisation for advice and guidance because a decision is outside your area of responsibility or the law. It is also about knowing how to explain to your customers the limitations of what you can do for them. Ignorance of the law is no excuse for failing to comply with the legal requirements so you need to demonstrate your continuous compliance with rules and regulations.

Knowledge evidence for Unit F2 (LO2)

As stated earlier, we will begin with learning outcome 2 (LO2). This contains the knowledge criteria for the unit and it is essential that you have this knowledge to underpin your performance. Note the assessment criteria in LO2 have been grouped into common themes and follow the cycle of the rules of customer service and therefore are not addressed in number sequence.

LO2 Know how to follow the rules to deliver customer service

Assessment criteria

2.1 Describe organisational practices and procedures that relate to their customer service work
2.2 Identify the limits of what they are allowed to do when delivering customer service
2.3 Explain when and how they should refer to somebody in authority about the rules for delivering customer service
2.4 Explain how they protect the security of customers and their property
2.5 Explain how they protect the security of information about customers
2.6 Describe their health and safety responsibilities as they relate to their customer service work
2.7 Explain their responsibilities to deliver customer service treating customers equally
2.8 Explain why it is important to respect customer and organisation confidentiality

2.9 List the main things they must do and not do in their job under legislation that affects their customer service work

2.10 List the main things that they must do and not do in their job under external regulations that affect their customer service work

TUTORIAL 1 with your virtual advisor:

Read through this tutorial so that you can meet the requirements of the assessment criteria shown above.

2.1 Describe organisational practices and procedures that relate to their customer service work

It is important that you are able to describe the procedures that you and your colleagues and service partners use at work when dealing with your internal and external customers and that you understand why they are there.

To recap:

● An internal customer is someone with whom you have contact, within your organisation. They could be the person who sits at the desk next to you or they could be in another department or location, but they are reliant on you providing them with products, processes or services.

● An external customer is anyone outside your organisation to whom you supply products or services.

● A service partner can be from another organisation or department and when you work together you will both help to provide more effective customer service. For example, a computer retailer might work with an IT help desk to provide after-care and a problem-solving service to a customer after purchase of the product.

The practices and procedures could relate to complaints, servicing or the delivery of goods and services. They could be working methods, for example, the housekeeping or cleaning processes at the beginning and end of a working day or shift, or the cash handling procedures. There will be some procedures that are directly relevant to your area of responsibility and others that require a general awareness.

Consider the following question in relation to your customer service situation. Making notes will help you to collect your thoughts and you can use them when you meet with your 'live' assessor or tutor.

Question

1. Make a list of three procedures that you have to use and describe how each one works.

2.2 Identify the limits of what they are allowed to do when delivering customer service

2.3 Explain when and how they should refer to somebody in authority about the rules for delivering customer service

It is important to understand the limits of your role and some of the ways you can do this include:

- an induction programme
- on-the-job training
- your job description
- your role profile
- one-to-one meetings or performance reviews with your manager
- through the experience of working with your customers.

If you are uninformed about products and services, customer service levels, rules and procedures, your objectives or targets and what you are allowed to do for your customer then the customer experience may be damaged or you might breach regulations or legislation. Some limits will evolve through your experience of dealing with customer problems and queries and the experience of team members. If you are unsure of the rules or what you are allowed to do for your customer, you must ask for advice and help from a more experienced colleague or service partner who is in a position of authority. Meetings and training sessions are good forums to discuss your questions and past experiences with others. This will enable you and your organisation to develop guidance about the limitations of what you can do when delivering customer service and who has the experience to make decisions about how the rules are followed. For example, a customer service professional in a retail environment would need to know the legal and organisational rules relating to customer refund periods.

In Chapter 7 (Unit C1) you will be asked to state the limits of what you are allowed to do when dealing with customer requests, queries or problems (assessment criteria 3.1, 3.2). Your answer for the knowledge criteria of Unit F2 may help you if you have selected Unit C1.

Now try the following questions in relation to your customer service situation. Making notes will help you to collect your thoughts and you can use them when you meet with your 'live' assessor or tutor.

Questions

1. List five things you can do and five things you cannot do in your customer service role.

2. How do you know the limits of your role? Where are these limits written?

3. Which person in authority would you ask for guidance or assistance in maintaining your organisation's rules?

4. Describe a customer transaction where you had to ask an experienced colleague about the rules for delivering customer service.

If you find it difficult to answer these questions you might find it useful to discuss them with your manager, supervisor or colleagues.

2.4 Explain how they protect the security of customers and their property

Whether you have to store customer information or property at certain times before, during or after a customer transaction will depend on the nature of the customer products or service that you and your organisation offer. The need to protect the security of a customer and their property might arise when they visit your organisation, for example, if you provide customer service to visitors to a leisure centre they might need to store their property in a secure place such as a locker while they are using a gym or swimming pool. Both you and your organisation are responsible for ensuring the locker is in good working order, secure and fit for the purpose of storing their property.

Most, if not all, visitors to an organisation will need to sign a register/visitors book and will be given a badge or identification pass. This is mainly to maintain security, as there might be confidential business being conducted or areas of no access, but it is also to ensure that your customer/visitor is accounted for in the event of an emergency such as a fire. If it is your responsibility, you must ensure you follow the rules of security of customers and their property at all times.

Now try the following questions in relation to your customer service situation.

Questions

1. What kind of property do you have to look after for your customers? If you are not required to look after property for your own customers, list three types of organisations where customer property is regularly handled, for example, a dry cleaning company.

2. What procedures do you have in place to protect customers and their property?

2.8 Explain why it is important to respect customer and organisation confidentiality

The need to protect the security of customers' information is widespread across an organisation. The customer might be internal or external and the information can range from personal things like their salary or bank details and date of birth, to product or intellectual property, project plans, inventions and ideas. You have an obligation to preserve the security and confidentiality of any information you hold for your customer if they tell you that this information should not be shared with others.

It is likely that you will store certain information electronically for your internal or external customers, in which case you should use password protection on your computer or electronic device (including a business use telephone) so that only you and other authorised personnel can access the information. The rules about giving this information will be communicated to you by your manager, the information technology (IT) or human resources (HR) department. You need to ensure you understand and use the guidance they provide.

Now try the following question in relation to your customer service situation.

Question

1. Why is it important to respect customer and organisation confidentiality?

2.5 Explain how they protect the security of information about customers

Confidentiality and security of personal information should be a matter of good practice but is also a legal requirement. The 1998 Data Protection Act (DPA) affects the handling and management of personal information belonging to both you and your customers. The DPA regulates all individually identifiable data relating to a living person and contained in a readily accessible filing system. The DPA covers not just electronically held data but also manually held data. There are eight enforceable principles for the obtaining, holding and disclosing of personal data. These principles, which must be complied with, state that the data must be:

1. *lawfully and fairly processed*: it has not been taken or processed without a customer's knowledge

2. *processed for specified purposes*: you must let your customer know why you are asking for the information and how you will use it

3. *adequate, relevant and not excessive*: only keep the information you need

4. *accurate and kept up to date*: you must regularly check and update the information for as long as you keep it

5. *not be kept for longer than is necessary*: have a review period so you are not keeping information unnecessarily

6. *processed within the rights of the data subject*: this means that the customer has the right to have the information about them removed

7. *held securely*: unauthorised people cannot access the information and you do not disclose information to others

8. *not transferred outside the EU to countries without adequate protection*: if customer information is going to be transferred or processed outside of the European Economic area it must be protected and the customer needs to be told that this will happen.

In summary, you must check procedures in your workplace for the protection of your customers' data and ensure that such information is only ever used for legitimate purpose. In effect, this means keeping it safe and not disclosing it to anyone outside of the organisation. Confidentiality and security are the key principles for you to observe.

Now try the following questions in relation to your customer service situation.

Questions

Research at least two application forms for a credit card and/or a bank account or an insurance policy (this can be online or in paper format).

1. Make a list of the types of information requested from the organisation which are covered by data protection.

2. What guarantees does the organisation give to the customer about the security of their information?

3. List the types of information that you request and hold for your customers.

4. Describe how you protect the security of information given to you by your customers.

2.6 Describe their health and safety responsibilities as they relate to their customer service work

Health and Safety at Work Act 1974

Health and safety at work is your responsibility as well as your manager's responsibility. Health and safety at work means preventing accidents, injuries and ill-health in the workplace. It means that you need to look out for both your own health and safety and that of your colleagues and customers. The Health and Safety at Work Act (HASWA) 1974 places duties on employers and employees. Employers are required to look after the safety of their employees by making sure that the workplace is safe and healthy, that the systems of work are safe and that tools, machinery, clothing and protective equipment are safe and fit for purpose. Importantly, the employer must ensure that employees and customers can safely evacuate the premises in an emergency.

Hazards and risks

As an employee you have duties too. You must cooperate with your employer in achieving a safe workplace and also take responsibility for your own safety and the safety of customers and other employees. Your employer must have a safety policy which states the organisation of and responsibilities for health and safety in the workplace, as well as the risks to health and safety which are present in that workplace. It is your responsibility to find out what the risks are and make every attempt to avoid injuring yourself. The Management of Health and Safety Regulations (1992, but consolidated in the Employment Rights Act of 1996, and subsequently) require employers to undertake risk assessments on a regular basis and report these findings to employees.

When undertaking a risk assessment, it is important to distinguish between a hazard and a risk. A hazard is something that has the potential to cause harm, for example, a sharp edge on a desk, a broken floor tile in the reception area or a computer chair that will not adjust to enable the person using the chair to set it to the correct height and back support. Clearly, it is important to identify hazards in the workplace, but equally important is establishing whether such a hazard is low, medium or high risk. This is established by considering each hazard against the following criteria:

- *Severity of harm*: how severe is the hazard in terms of the likely injury: will it be a cut finger or a severe head injury?

- *Likelihood of harm*: the probability of the hazard hurting someone. A broken floor tile against a wall or under a table is less likely to cause injury than one in a main doorway in reception.

- *The number of people at risk*: for example, if a workstation chair (used by a number of internal customers or service partners) is not adjustable, but it still fits the two customers who use it, it remains a hazard, but the risk to health and safety is low. However, if the chair does not fit ten users, then the number of people at risk becomes high.

As a customer service professional it is important that you take responsibility for identifying the hazards and assess the risks to you, your fellow workers and your customers in your workplace – it is your responsibility as well as that of your manager.

Figure F2.2

Accident prevention

Accidents and injuries can happen anywhere and at any time and it is part of your job to take safety precautions to prevent accidents and injuries. Often accidents occur because a person is inexperienced or working in unfamiliar surroundings or unable to recognise unsafe acts or situations. They may lack knowledge or be too embarrassed to ask questions. As a customer service professional concerned with providing an excellent customer service environment, safe working practices must be a priority. Use your risk assessment skills to identify, reduce, eliminate or report hazards.

Proper health and safety awareness is the key to reducing accidents and work-related ill-health. Under health and safety law and regulations your employer should provide training in the following areas:

- fire safety – prevention, extinguishing and emergency exits
- what to do in an emergency
- potential for violent or abusive behaviour from customers or clients
- first aid arrangements

- procedure for reporting accidents and knowledge of RIDDOR (Reporting of Injuries, Diseases and Dangerous Occurrences Regulations 1995)
- good housekeeping – cleanliness and tidiness
- electrical safety
- safety signs and symbols and what they mean
- personal protective equipment (PPE)
- hazardous substances (COSSH) – see below
- manual handling – see below
- display screen equipment (DSE) – see below.

COSSH

The Control of Substances Hazardous to Health (COSSH) Regulations 1992 provide guidance on the handling and storage of substances such as chemicals, paints, solvents, bacteria, infectious diseases and fumes.

Manual handling

Manual handling is a particularly important area because most people undertake some form of manual handling in their work and poor manual handling can result in permanent musculoskeletal damage. There are correct ways to twist, bend, lift, carry and place in relation to load size, shape, weight and distance to be carried. You need to be particularly diligent in learning how to undertake safe lifting and carrying and should ask yourself questions such as:

1. What weight is this load and is it within my capacity?

2. Is the load an awkward shape?

3. Does it have sharp edges?

4. Where do I need to take the load and are there any steps, slopes or obstacles?

5. Are any mechanical lifting aids available?

If you do this you will be engaging in dynamic risk assessment each time you consider manual handling and this has the potential to protect you from risk. For example, you might consider it necessary for a trolley to be provided or another means of moving goods from dispatch to transport, so that you or your customers do not get injured lifting. Not only is this taking account of the risks customers could be exposed to but it also provides an additional customer service.

Personal protective equipment (PPE)

PPE such as steel toe capped shoes, safety helmets, goggles and ear defenders are items that must be provided where the risks are judged to make them necessary. Your responsibility is to use them as instructed and take care of them.

Display screen equipment (DSE)

DSE refers to a computer with a screen, keyboard and mouse. DSE can affect the body as computer use often involves sitting still for long periods, leading to fatigue because the brain and eyes have to concentrate on the screen, and repetitive strain injuries. It is important for you and your employer to assess your DSE workstation in relation to seating, eye level and distance, reflective glare, screen angles, screen brightness and contrast, room lighting, mouse techniques and desk arrangements. Regular breaks should be taken to avoid spending long periods in the same position. You and your manager should identify what training you need to enable you to learn how to sit properly and you should be able to adjust your office furniture to increase your comfort level and avoid over stretching and strains.

It should be clear by now that health and safety is a serious matter even in what might be considered low risk environments, such as shops, offices and call contact centres. If health and safety is not a priority then the consequences to you and your organisation might be:

● injuries and ill-health for employees and customers

● legal consequences, because you and your employer might be fined by the Health and Safety Executive enforcement officers

● financial costs to the organisation from loss of business

● negative impact on the reputation of the organisation.

For an abundance of useful information on health and safety, go to the Health and Safety Executive website: **www.hse.gov.uk**

Now try the following question in relation to your customer service situation.

Question

1. Highlight two examples of your health and safety responsibilities and how they relate to your role as customer service professional.

2.7 Explain their responsibilities to deliver customer service treating customers equally

The Equality Act 2010 established the concept of 'protected characteristics' relating to:

● age

● disability

● gender reassignment

● marriage and civil partnership

● pregnancy and maternity

● race, religion or belief

● sex

● sexual orientation.

The Equality Act 2010 incorporates the principles from the Disability Discrimination Acts, 1995 and 2005. Under the terms of the Act protection is provided against unreasonable or unfavourable treatment through direct and indirect discrimination on the basis of a protected characteristic. It is therefore unlawful to treat people with these protected characteristics in anyway less favourably than people who do not share these characteristics. Your organisation will have policies in relation to equality of opportunity, the prevention of unlawful discrimination and the promotion of diversity. Find out about these and be sure of your responsibilities.

A good customer service professional will, however, make reasonable adjustments for people with disabilities. Although the stereotypical image of a disabled person is someone in a wheelchair, this is not the only type of disability covered by the law. Disability organisation estimate that only around 5 per cent of people with disabilities need to use a wheelchair. Many other disabilities are covered by the law, including visual and hearing impairment or loss, and learning difficulties. The Equality Act 2010 confers statutory rights and some limited protection against discrimination to people with disabilities. The Act defines disability as 'a physical or mental impairment which has a substantial and long-term adverse effect on a person's ability to carry out normal day-to-day activities'.

The Act places a responsibility on employers and providers of goods and services to make reasonable adjustments for people with disabilities. Your employer will have in place a policy on the treatment of people with disabilities in terms of access to goods and services. It is your responsibility as a customer service professional to understand ways in which people with disabilities may have different customer service needs and to try to meet those needs. In addition to mobility disabilities, other disabilities that you may need to accommodate relate to visual or hearing impairment or loss and learning difficulties.

Figure F2.3: Meeting the needs of all your customers

We all learn at different rates and it is important to adjust your explanations about your goods and services to the learning capacity of the individual customer. Always check out levels of understanding if you pick up any verbal or non-verbal cues about the extent to which you customer understands or does not understand what you are saying. Check your organisation's equal opportunity policy and familiarise yourself with how it works in practice.

Now try the following questions. Making notes will help you to collect your thoughts and you can use them when you meet with your 'live' assessor or tutor.

Questions

1. When you are out and about as a customer, observe and make notes of how organisations such as retailers, banks and restaurant/cafes make adjustments for:
   - customers with mobility disabilities
   - customers with visual impairments
   - customers with hearing loss
   - customers with learning difficulties
   - mothers and babies
   - elderly customers.

2. What adjustments do you and your organisation make for:
   - customers with mobility disabilities
   - customers with visual impairments
   - customers with hearing loss
   - customers with learning difficulties
   - mothers and babies
   - elderly customers.

2.9 List the main things they must do and not do in their job under legislation that affects their customer service work

2.10 List the main things that they must do and not do in their job under external regulations that affect their customer service work

There is a difference between legislation and regulations. Legislation is a directive put in place by government or industry which must be complied with to stay within the law. An example is the health and safety law that has already been discussed in this chapter. When laws are in place, the detail of how the law will be enforced will be decided by a group of people (usually a government department). A regulation is set by an organisation or a sector and is usually linked to legislation. The following is an example of the difference between legislation and regulation: The Health Bill was presented to the government and made provision for smoking to be banned on certain premises and places. This became law in 2007. When this came into force every organisation in England and Wales had to have regulations (and policies) in place for their staff and customers in order to comply with the law.

So far we have looked at three areas of legislation that must be taken into consideration in any job role in any organisation:

1. Health and Safety
2. Data Protection
3. Equality of opportunity

Depending on the sector that you work within, there may be other legislation that you must also be aware of. For example, a customer service professional working as a:

● supermarket retailer: under the terms of the Offensive Weapons Act 1996, it is illegal to sell knives or blades to people under the age of 18 years. It Is also an offence to sell alcohol to young people under the age of 18 years or to a person acting on behalf of the young person

● delivery driver: the Road Traffic Act 1991 requires compliance with road safety.

The external regulations that will affect the same customer service professionals are:

● retailer: regulations about the sale of knives and blades or alcohol (particularly in a supermarket) will detail where they are displayed and stored, the training of staff and other important issues

● delivery driver: the regulations for road drivers are found in the Highway Code, and relate to road safety advice, speeds, signs and road markings and right of way.

Consider the following questions in relation to your customer service situation. Making notes will help you to collect your thoughts and you can use them when you meet with your 'live' assessor or tutor.

Questions

1. List the main things you must do and must not do in your customer service work linked to legislation.

2. List the main things that you must do and must not do in your customer service work linked to external regulations.

This tutorial has looked at the legislation and regulations that will have a bearing on what you can and cannot do for your customers. This will influence your procedures and the rules put in place by your organisation.

The case study section provides an opportunity for you to read about a customer service professional or scenario. The case study consolidates some of the information from the tutorial. You can use this to reflect on the situation and answer some questions. Again, you do not have to write your answers down unless your tutor or assessor has asked you to do so.

Candice is an ex-nurse and works in a call centre for a health helpline service. On a regular shift she will handle a number of calls from her customers, members of the public, who have health concerns but are reluctant to call an ambulance and cannot get to their local GP. Candice's knowledge of nursing comes in very useful and there are stringent guidelines relating to what she can and cannot advise a customer to do and when she must contact her service partners or colleagues for help.

The call centre has staff working 24 hours a day, seven days a week. The desks are shared, so when Candice arrives for work she has to adjust her chair and the height of her desk and clean down her workstation with sterilising wipes. She collects her headphones and logs into her computer using a password because the information that she keeps is highly confidential.

Some of the customers are distressed and anxious and Candice ensures that she deals with all of them according to their needs. She only asks questions that are absolutely necessary and she is careful how she records the information on her database. She processes the calls and uses the information she has onscreen to advise her customers. If she assesses that a customer is vulnerable or in danger she will call the emergency services but if not she makes referrals to GP practices or deals with the situation herself over the phone.

Candice has clear regulations and guidelines about what she can and cannot do for her customers and these are all documented. For example, she cannot prescribe medicines and if a customer has a particular pre-existing condition she must make sure a paramedic is called immediately to go and assess the situation. From time to time she has to get information from her team leader, if she does not know the answer to a query or problem. Candice undertakes regular training and meetings to make sure she is up to date with any new legislation, regulations or procedures.

After each call Candice completes the relevant documentation so that others can see a record of what has occurred and to cover her if anything goes wrong and there is an enquiry into the incident. Occasionally a customer will have special requirements and she will adjust her service to suit them. She has a special telephone system for people with hearing loss or who are deaf: they are able to text their questions through on a textphone service. She also has access to interpreters for people who do not speak or understand English.

Candice is expected to provide a service that matches the organisation's published vision to be an effective and efficient healthline, providing expert heath information and reassurance through a first class telephone line and website and other digitally delivered health services.

Questions

1. What legislation, rules and procedures does Candice have to think about when she is working with her customers?

2. How does Candice prepare for her shift and what health and safety checks and actions does she take?

3. How does Candice keep her knowledge, of what she can and cannot do in her customer service role, up to date?

4. How does Candice protect the health and safety of her customers?

5. What precautions does Candice take to maintain security and confidentiality of information?

The reflective activity below is designed to help you to start thinking about your reactions and feelings when you encounter different customer service scenarios. We are all customers on a regular basis, and this activity is from the perspective of you as the customer and as the customer service professional. It will help to prepare you to collect evidence that will demonstrate your knowledge, understanding and practical skills in customer service. Write down your reflections if you wish as they may be useful in discussions or sessions with your assessor or in the preparation of evidence.

REFLECTIVE ACTIVITY 1

Analyse a recent experience when you were the customer and the customer service professional asked you for personal or confidential information.

1. What was the information and why did they require it?
2. How did they explain what they needed and why they needed the information?
3. What reassurances did they give to you that the information would not be shared with others?
4. How did you feel about the way they handled the situation?

Now analyse a recent experience when you were the customer service professional and you had to ask a customer for personal or confidential information.

1. What was the information and why did you require it?
2. How did you explain what you needed and why you needed the information?
3. What reassurances did you give to your customer that the information would not be shared with others?
4. How did your customer react towards your request for the information?
5. How could you make improvements to the way you requested the information in the future?

If you cannot think of your own examples, speak to a friend, colleague or your tutor and ask them about theirs.

Performance evidence for Unit F2 (LO1)

The case study so far has given you the opportunity to consider the rules that Candice follows in her customer service setting. The reflective activity has enabled you to look at the rules relating to the customer service experience that you have received from others as well as the rules relating to the service that you deliver to your customers.

The next section in this unit is designed to help you focus on the learning outcomes and performance requirement of Unit F2 and prompt you to think how you can evidence this through your customer service role. It is expected that the evidence that you generate for this unit will also cross-reference with some of the optional units that you have selected. The virtual advisor will guide you to collect the evidence that you need to complete this unit.

Performance evidence is different from knowledge evidence and requires you to identify events that have happened in the course of your job in a real work environment. You will have to prove that the customers really exist and the events or incidents really happened – your assessor will help you to do this. The ways that you can present the evidence will be explained in Tutorial 2 below. You should answer the questions in the context of where you work and your provision of customer service. This time it *is* important for you to record your answers in writing as this will be the foundation of your evidence. However, you need only write notes to remind you where the proof is located.

LO1 Follow their organisation's customer service practices and procedures

F1.3 Assessment criteria

1.1 Follow organisational practices and procedures that relate to their customer service work
1.2 Recognise the limits of what they are allowed to do when delivering customer service
1.3 Refer to somebody in authority when they need to
1.4 Work in a way that protects the security of customers and their property
1.5 Work in a way that protects the security of information about customers

TUTORIAL 2 with your virtual advisor:

This tutorial is not intended to take the place of meetings with your assessor but to offer some support and a refresher in his or her absence.

Much of the knowledge supporting the assessment criteria in this section has been discussed in learning outcome 2 earlier in this chapter. You were asked to provide some examples of the procedures that you use when you are providing customer service, the limits of your job role and who to go to if you need to ask for guidance. You also looked at the laws and regulations that underpin everything you have to do for your customer, especially those related to health and safety, data protection and equality. In addition, you identified further legislation and regulations specific to your own sector or organisation.

The evidence you need to produce for this unit could be an observation by your assessor of you working and interacting with your customers and colleagues. Use the ideas or notes that you have already made for learning outcome 2 to prepare for a professional discussion or a personal statement/case study (verbal or written) with your assessor. Evidence will need to be supported by work products like the documentation you complete for the customers, the procedures that you use, customer databases or quality checks carried out on your work by colleagues or managers. The evidence that you present should cover as many of the assessment criteria for this unit as possible and cross-reference to some of your optional units.

In some cases you will not be able to include work product evidence because of confidentiality or data protection regulations. In this instance you can ask your manager or a colleague to confirm that they have seen your work or you have participated in discussions and/or meetings.

Evidence requirements provide the context in which you meet the assessment criteria for performance and will enable your assessor to judge whether you are competent in a number of different situations. You do not need to cover the evidence requirements separately; they will be covered as you complete the assessment criteria. Your assessor will give you guidance. The evidence requirements for Unit F2 are explained in Tutorial 3 below.

TUTORIAL 3 with your virtual advisor:

You must provide evidence of following the rules to deliver customer service:

- *During routine delivery of customer service*: This is when you are working under normal circumstances, i.e. not under extra pressure or dealing with unusual circumstances like holiday periods or seasonal surges (such as during national holidays). (It is up to you to establish what is normal!)

- *During a busy time in your job:* Once you have decided on what is the routine delivery of customer service, you will be able to identify your busy times. You need to show that you look after the safety and security of your customers even when you are under pressure. Often you will be aware of the times when you are going to be busy and can take this into consideration when selecting opportunities for your evidence collection.

- *During a quiet time in your job:* In the same way you identified busy times in your job, you should also identify when quiet times occur. Do you find things to do or do you sit around looking bored? Think about the activities that you carry out when there is some downtime. Perhaps this is the time that you catch up on paperwork, cleaning and maintenance, health and safety checks or carry out development activities and meetings.

- *When people, systems or resources have let you down:* Often we are not aware that other people in the customer service chain have let us down until the customer has made us aware that things have gone wrong. How often does your computer crash or go slow or the printer run out of paper at a crucial time in the customer service transaction? These are the types of circumstances that you are likely to encounter that will meet this evidence requirement. Do you get anxious or stressed or even a bit short with the customer? It is important to ensure that you still follow the rules under these circumstances. You need to demonstrate calm and business-like behaviour and should not cut corners or let things slip. Accidents can happen when people are frustrated or angry so that is the time to take more care.

Performance evidence activity 1

Provide a written example of how you follow your organisation's customer service practices and procedures in each of the following circumstances:

- routine delivery of customer service
- a busy time in your job
- a quiet time in your job
- when people, systems or resources have let you down.

One of the examples should show that you have recognised the limits of what you are allowed to do and have referred to somebody in authority when delivering customer service. All examples should demonstrate that you have worked in a way that protects the security (of information or property) and the safety of your customers. The examples will be the foundation of your evidence for this and other units.

LEARNER EVALUATION ACTIVITY

The last activity is the learner evaluation. Each section in this chapter is intended to help you to develop yourself towards being a more thinking and reflective customer service professional. The learner evaluation requires you to reflect on your learning from completing this unit guide. Once again, this does not have to be written; however, it could be very useful to record your answers for use in reviews with your line manager, supervisor, assessor or tutor or possibly in a job interview.

Documenting your learning throughout your working life is a very effective way of showing that you use experience to influence your performance and behaviours. Reflect on what you knew at the start of the unit and what you know now.

1. What have you learned from completing this unit?
2. Identify three phrases that were new to you.
3. How will completing this unit affect your customer service within your organisation?
4. Highlight an improvement that you have made as a result of completing this unit.

If you are working towards Unit D3 Develop personal performance through delivering customer service, your evaluations might also provide you with some foundation evidence.

Summary

This concludes the unit guidance for Unit F2 Follow the rules to deliver customer service.

You should be prepared to submit evidence for both the knowledge and performance aspects of the unit learning outcomes:

LO1: Follow their organisation's customer service practices and procedures
LO2: Know how to follow the rules to deliver customer service

You will now be able to describe how you follow the rules of your organisation to deliver customer service to your internal and external customers. This will include following all relevant procedures and processes in your organisation.

It is likely that the knowledge and performance evidence you produce for this unit will cross-reference to the following Customer Service units:

● Unit A10 Deal with customers face to face

● Unit A11 Deal with incoming telephone calls from customers

● Unit B2 Deliver reliable customer service

● Unit D1 Develop customer relationships

● Unit C1 Recognise and deal with customer queries, requests and problems

● Unit F1 Communicate using customer service language

GIVE CUSTOMERS A POSITIVE IMPRESSION OF YOURSELF AND YOUR ORGANISATION

Learning outcomes

> **Learning outcomes for Unit A4:**
> 1. Establish rapport with customers
> 2. Respond appropriately to customers
> 3. Communicate information to customers
> 4. Understand how to give customers a positive impression of themselves and the organisation

This unit guide is a resource to help you gather the evidence that you will require to achieve Unit A4, one of the optional units in the 'Impression and image' theme of the Level 2 NVQ Certificate in Customer Service. It can be used as a learning resource if you are new to your role, are studying customer service in preparation for work or as a refresher if you are an experienced customer service professional.

Give customers a positive impression of yourself and your organisation – what is Unit A4 about?

Unit A4 is about:

… communicating with the customer and giving a positive impression whenever dealing with a customer.

… how you can create a positive impression of the organisation and the customer service it provides. All of us enjoy the experience of good customer service if we feel that the person serving us really wants to create the right impression, responds to us and gives us good information. Every detail of your behaviour counts when dealing with the customer.

Source: Adapted from Unit A4 purpose and aim

You will be able to demonstrate how you establish rapport with your customers, how you respond appropriately to customers and how you communicate information to them. You should be able to understand and explain how to give your customers a positive impression of yourself and the methods of communication that you use in your organisation to enable you to carry this out effectively.

Completing this unit guide

To complete this unit guide you will need to:

1. Read through the information in each section
2. Look at the case study and reflective activities and use the questions to help you to test your understanding.

There is no set format for working through or recording your answers in these sections, just use them in a way that suits your learning style, unless otherwise instructed by your assessor or tutor. The case study and reflective activities are linked to the assessment criteria in learning outcome 4, which focuses on the underpinning knowledge and understanding for Unit A4. Learning outcome 4 has been presented first so that you understand the background to the criteria in learning outcomes 1, 2 and 3. If you work through this section first you will find that your performance evidence will be easier to identify and present to your assessor.

Learning outcome 4 – Knowledge evidence

LO4 Understand how to give customers a positive impression of themselves and the organisation

- The tutorial section is designed to explain the assessment criteria. In this section your virtual advisor will provide you with information to help you interpret the national standards.

- The case study and reflective activities will help you to prepare to discuss and explain your understanding of customer service with your assessor.

Learning outcomes 1, 2 and 3 – Performance evidence

LO1 Establish rapport with customer
LO2 Respond appropriately to customers
LO3 Communicate information to customers

In addition to the learning outcomes, in this unit there are **evidence requirements** that indicate the circumstances or conditions under which you should present the evidence.

- Your communication with customers may be face-to-face, in writing, by telephone, text message, e-mail, Internet (including social networking), intranet or by any other method you would be expected to use within your job role.

You must provide evidence of creating a positive impression with customers:

- during routine delivery of customer service
- during a busy time in your job
- during a quiet time in your job
- when people, systems or resources have let you down.

You must provide evidence that you communicate effectively by:

- using appropriate spoken or written language
- applying the conventions and rules appropriate to the methods of communication you have chosen.

In all three learning outcomes the performance evidence activities, assisted by your virtual assessor, will help you reflect on your performance and knowledge as a customer service professional and will enable you to identify and gather evidence.

Why do I need to give customers a positive impression of myself and my organisation?

Customer service is not just a job; it underpins everything you do in your work role. If you are involved in providing products or services to others, internal or external to your organisation, it is essential that you are able to:

- communicate in a way that meets the needs of the customer
- behave in a manner that is suitable for the situation and the customer.

The cycle of communication

The cycle of communication (Figure 3.1) illustrates four important stages of communication in any customer service transaction.

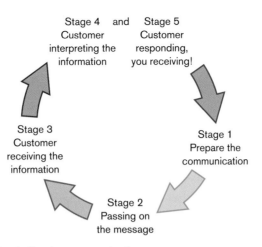

Figure A4.1: The cycle of effective communication

On the surface, communication seems quite straightforward: you have a message or information that you need to convey to another person or group of people. You are the sender and in the context of this chapter the receiver is an internal or external customer. This communication might contain simple or complex information, so what could go wrong? You will know from personal experience that many things can interfere with your communication and impair the end result. This can happen in your home and business life and the outcome can affect relationships in a number of ways.

The cycle of excellent communication breaks down the stages of any communication, whether it is a simple or complex transaction, so you can understand and plan how to use the most appropriate method of communication for your customer.

Stage 1 Prepare the communication

Prepare the communication for the receiver (your customer). This is possibly the most important part in the cycle and it is vital to get this right first time.

- Deciding what you will put into the communication is essential. Consider the organisation procedures for written communication and follow the rules (formal or informal). If you are using verbal communication (either face to face or over the telephone), there may be company protocols or legal information that you have to convey before you continue the rest of the conversation. You should also consider the order in which you will provide the information.

- What do you need to get out of the communication? Are you asking the customer to supply information or telling them about a delivery date or letting them know some facts or figures? If the news is unlikely to meet their expectations then think about how you can present this in a more positive light.

- Consider who is going to receive your communication and if possible think about their needs and how they will react to the message.

Stage 2 Passing on the message

The second stage is when you convert stage 1 into action and pass on the message to your customer. Before you do so, consider the following:

● Is it the right time and circumstance to do this? Think about the external and internal interferences that might be present to the customer. For example, they could be driving and not be able to concentrate, or they might be rushing off to collect their children, or in a noisy restaurant or shopping centre.

● Will the customer understand the language that you are using? Think about their personality or preferences, if you have that information.

● Analyse the way you are delivering the message. Listen to the speed at which you are speaking – do you sound irritated or stressed? Consider your body language and facial expressions as these can be conveyed to the receiver even if you are speaking on the telephone. If it is an email, review the written word and check your spelling and grammar before you click on 'send'.

● Think about the quantity of information that you are delivering and make sure that you provide it in digestible chunks.

Stage 3 Customer receiving the information

At this point in the cycle you have lost some of the control. You have sent the message and it is down to the receiver (the customer) to now interpret and analyse what you have delivered. However, at this point you may also become the receiver and in this case you will need to exercise 'active listening'. This involves:

● listening or reading carefully the response to your communication, without interruption

● looking out for body language or written clues that might indicate misinterpretation or lack of understanding

● asking the sender to explain if you do not understand what they mean or are saying

● providing encouraging responses or body language to the customer.

Stage 4 Customer interpreting the information

Stage 5 Customer responding, you receiving

At stages 4 and 5 in the cycle, both you and the customer could be senders and receivers and this is where it gets complicated. Both parties are now trying to make sense of what each other are saying. It is therefore essential you:

● match the way that you send and receive the message to the needs of the customer

● pick up clues from their responses each time you interact and use these to understand a little more about them

● have an awareness of issues of gender, experience, language, personal preferences and priorities relating to their needs.

And so the cycle starts again …

Knowledge evidence for Unit A4 (LO4)

This section is designed to support you and to take an in-depth look at the assessment criteria in each learning outcome.

As stated earlier, we will begin with learning outcome 4 (LO4). This contains the knowledge criteria for the unit. In order to sustain and improve in your role as a customer service professional it is essential that you have this knowledge to underpin your performance.

You may be very competent in customer service but unless you understand your organisation's standards, guidelines, rules, procedures and methods of effective communication with customers you cannot move to the next level of professionalism. You also need to understand some of the theory of customer transactions and how to deal with different types of customers and their needs and wants. This tutorial will provide some background to these areas and help you to research and obtain information that is not only relevant to your current role but also similar roles in other organisations.

LO4 Understand how to give customers a positive impression of themselves and the organisation

Assessment criteria

4.1 Describe their organisation's standards for appearance and behaviour
4.2 Explain their organisation's guidelines for how to recognise what their customer wants and respond appropriately
4.3 Identify their organisation's rules and procedures regarding the methods of communication they use

Figure A4.2: First impressions count

TUTORIAL 1 with your virtual advisor:

Read through this tutorial so that you can meet the requirements of the first three assessment criteria shown above.

4.1 Describe their organisation's standards for appearance and behaviour

First impressions count with a customer and they can make or break an organisation's reputation. You might be the only person that the customer has contact with, so how you appear and behave (whether auditory, visually or remotely) will have an impact on their perception of the organisation.

All organisations have their own standards for appearance and behaviour. Some are more formal than others and this often depends on the customer base. For example, a sound technician working at a radio station will interact with a number of internal and external customers within the music industry and perhaps with local businesses. The dress and personal presentation of the customers will vary according to the genre of music or the organisation that they represent and the dress code within the radio station may therefore reflect this.

Standards of behaviour and language will vary depending on the customer base; what is deemed acceptable to internal customers might need to be adjusted when dealing with external customers. This is explained in more detail in Chapter 1 Unit F1.

Behaviour in any business context needs to be kept in line with legal obligations and decency. Very few employers allow their employees to swear or to treat others in an offensive manner, whether face to face, verbally or in writing. All people in the UK are covered by the Equality Act, which came into force on 1 October 2010. There are a number of areas within the Act that are linked to how an individual behaves both inside and outside the work environment and how people are treated by others. Take some time to look at the Act and also at the policies in your organisation relating to equal opportunities and diversity that are influenced by the legislation. (Legislation is covered in more detail in Chapter 2 Unit F2.)

You will need to consider other policies and procedures that are in place in your organisation. These might include rules relating to the wearing of jewellery, hair styles, bullying, swearing and personal protection. Many of these policies are in place to preserve and enhance the wellbeing of both the customer service professional and the customer.

Many customer service professionals are expected to wear some type of personal identity (e.g. name badge or ID card) and corporate business dress or uniform. Rules related to this can be very strict as they are often linked to the security of staff and customers. It is vital that you find out what the rules, requirements and boundaries are in your organisation and comply with them.

There may be policies and procedures related to smoking and the use of alcohol and drugs at work. These are generally in place because of laws (European and UK) and also consideration for colleagues and customers.

Other policies may refer to the personal use of a computer at work (including the use of social networks) and many employers will not allow this in work time (sometimes in personal time at work as well). Recently a number of employees have found themselves in trouble with their employer, colleagues or customers because they have posted inappropriate remarks on their social networking site, forgetting that the posts are increasingly in the public domain. In extreme circumstances the comments can be seen as bullying, discriminatory or a breach of security.

Consider the following questions in relation to communication with customers. Making notes will help you to collect your thoughts and you can use them when you meet with your 'live' assessor or tutor. If you cannot find any information in your own organisation, you may be able to ask a friend or family member who is in a workplace.

Questions

1. Where could an employee find out about standards of appearance at work?

2. List some of the standards.

3. Where can an employee locate information about standards of behaviour at work?

4. List and explain at least two workplace policies linked to how a customer service professional is expected to behave towards internal and external customers (e.g. use of email or social networking sites).

5. How could such policies affect how they behave?

6. What standards of behaviour or appearance are in place because of health and safety or security?

To sum up, it is essential that even if there are no written rules or regulations regarding appearance and behaviour, you must find out what is acceptable within your organisation. If nothing already exists this could be discussed with your manager and colleagues so that you can set appropriate guidelines.

4.2 Explain their organisation's guidelines for how to recognise what their customer wants and respond appropriately

You must be able to explain your organisation's guidelines for identifying what your customers want and need. You can do this by finding out exactly what your organisation currently promises, offers and delivers to its customers. You looked at ways that this can be achieved in Chapter 1 Unit F1 (assessment criteria 3.4 and 3.5). You also need to be able to explain where such information can be found. If you have difficulty in accessing this information, talk to your manager or supervisor and ask them where you can locate it. Alternatively, you may be able to work-shadow a more experienced colleague to find out this information.

Every day we exchange hundreds of words and many of these exchanges will be with your customers. One way you can recognise what a customer wants is by practising good listening skills, often referred to as 'active listening'. When a customer says something you must not only listen to what they say but also interpret the meaning of what they are saying to you. This is a very complex skill and often our attention drifts or we start overlaying our own understanding of what they are saying or even worse interrupting with our own version. When this happens we often miss part of the information being relayed to us. The art of active listening is to give your full attention before analysing what has been said. Once your customer has finished you then have the opportunity to check your interpretation of what they have said by asking questions.

You should look for clues from your customers in the smaller detail of what they are saying; often a customer will drop a comment into conversation which might indicate they are less than happy with the service received, or that they have not been able to get exactly what they were looking for. These are clues that help you to identify their needs both now and in the future. In a case such as this, you can demonstrate active listening by repeating the main points of your customer's conversation in your own words to show you have understood them.

Another important part of active listening is to use positive body language. This can be as simple as facing the person and nodding now and then, or if on the telephone by making short comments to show you are listening. Even on the telephone body language is important as this can be conveyed in your voice. Therefore, always remember to smile slightly or have a warm friendly approach and convey a willingness to help.

Products and services are changing so fast that customers sometimes do not even know what exists to meet their needs. Communications technology is a very good example: a customer might be looking for a mobile phone but it will not be until a customer service professional starts to ask questions and listen to what the customer is saying that they can ascertain the features and benefits that might be right for that customer. (See also Chapter 1 Unit F1, assessment criterion 3.2.)

Make time to discuss with your manager and colleagues what your customers think of your service or products. You should not take a lack of customer reaction as an indication of satisfaction – if you do not get complaints or feedback it might be because your customers cannot be bothered to complain. Often this can be more damaging to your organisation than receiving a complaint, because these customers will tell friends and family but you will not have an opportunity to put the problem right for them.

You need to be proactive and ask whether the customer is happy with the customer service provided. This could be informally by asking a customer whether the report you provided last week gave them all the information they needed, or whether they were happy with the time for delivery. A more formal way could be to invite a customer to complete a short survey and ask them for improvement suggestions. Being proactive is more than just knowing about the products and service that you can offer; it is about how you react to each customer that you come into contact with.

Consider the following questions in relation to communication with your customers. Making notes might help you to collect your thoughts and you can use them when you meet with your assessor or tutor.

Questions

Take some time out over the next week to actively listen to your customers. Select three transactions, listen out for clues and identify and record three comments the customer makes that could be used to improve the way you meet your customers' needs.

1. How can you use the comments to improve your customer service?

2. Who will you discuss the comments with to share good practice?

4.3 Identify their organisation's rules and procedures regarding the methods of communication they use

The following methods of communication are widely used in organisations and it is important that you have an understanding of the rules and procedures that surround them:

- verbal communication
- written communication
- non-verbal communication.

Verbal communication includes:

- Face-to-face
- Telephone
- One-to-one meetings
- Meetings
- Electronic conferencing (e.g. Skype), video conferencing.

Written communication includes:

- email
- text
- letters
- internet and intranet (including social networking sites)
- posters/adverts
- instant mail/chat rooms
- blogs and Tweets.

Non-verbal communication includes:

- eye contact
- facial expression
- body language
- sign language.

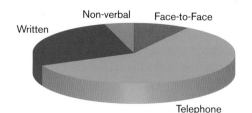

Figure A4.3: Pie chart showing different types of communication used by a call centre worker

Figure 3.2 shows the types of communication used in a call centre worker's role in the form of a pie chart. She spends 55 per cent of her working day speaking to people on the telephone outside the organisation or in other departments; occasionally (10 per cent) she uses face-to-face communication; 30 per cent of her time is taken up recording information on her PC (emails, updating databases and personal records of her customers) the remaining 5 per cent of her time is non-verbal communication when she is interacting with her internal customers face-to-face. In this example the time has only been divided into the main categories of communication, but it would be possible to analyse each category further by examining the methods of communication used within each category.

REFLECTIVE ACTIVITY 1

Think of the communication methods that you personally use in your organisation. How much time do you take from your working day using each of the following methods?

- Verbal communication
- Written communication
- Non-verbal communication

Draw a diagram showing the percentage of time you spend on each of the methods of communication you use in your organisation.

Questions

1. What method do you use the most?
2. What methods are the most effective for your customers?
3. What can go wrong with your communications?
4. Which is the least effective method for you and why?
5. How can you improve your methods of communication? (Ask your manager or supervisor to give you some feedback and help.)

Now read the case study below and answer the questions that follow to consolidate some of the information covered in Tutorial 1. Once again, you do not have to write your answers down unless your tutor or assessor has asked you to do so.

CASE STUDY 1 Liz and the show shop

Liz works in a specialist shoe retailer in a busy shopping outlet. It is Sunday and nearly 5.00 p.m. It has been a tedious afternoon with lots of customers coming in trying on shoes and asking lots of questions. Liz is tired; the weather outside is lovely and she wants to go home to sit in the garden. In addition she has torn the edge of her T shirt on one of the fixtures and she is feeling dusty and hot. She cannot be bothered to smile at the customers coming in and has given up on the greeting that her company says she is supposed to give when customers come in.

The shop has a lot of ex-sample shoes for sale today and these are displayed on tables with a sign to say how much they are and a note about the returns policy. Liz has been told that company policy states that samples cannot be returned or exchanged.

A customer comes up with a pair of shoes and wants to purchase them. Liz enters the transaction at the point of sale and as she does so she once again states the policy on sample returns and gives the customer a piece of paper with some very small print. The customer looks at the sheet of paper and explains that she has forgotten her reading glasses and could Liz read it out to her. Liz does so, speaking very fast. When she finishes the customer asks, with a smile on her face, if the no returns policy applies if the shoes are faulty and the sole falls off. Liz says very abruptly 'yes' and exasperatedly repeats the policy to the customer. The customer is a bit taken aback and becomes a bit defensive, quoting consumer rights and goods not being fit for purpose. Immediately Liz thinks to herself, we have a know-it all here and she raises her voice slightly as she says 'it's company policy and I have to keep to it'. She immediately sees that the customer has started to get a bit annoyed. The customer retaliates by saying that if the merchandise is faulty then she would have a right to a refund or repair. Liz starts to get annoyed – all she wants to do is complete the transaction. She says in an aggressive tone 'that will be £99 please'. The customer looks even more taken aback and says 'I thought they were only £70' and points to a ticket inside the shoe. Liz looks, gives an enormous sigh of frustration and then says that this is the cost price from the warehouse and can't the customer see that the price is on the ticket on the display table? Liz folds her arms and the customer looks very upset saying she did not see the price as she has not got her glasses. She says she is not prepared to take the risk on the shoes as they are nearly £100. She leaves the shop looking very disappointed. Liz shrugs her shoulders and thinks 'silly woman, can't she read!' and thinks about going home to her garden.

Questions

1. At what points during the transaction did things go wrong with Liz's behaviour?
2. What action could Liz have taken to try to meet her customer's needs?
3. How could Liz have changed the outcome of this transaction with her customer?
4. What information should Liz check out a) with her organisation b) on a consumer rights website or the Office of Fair Trading?
5. How could she have communicated this to her customer?

LO4 Understand how to give customers a positive impression of themselves and the organisation

Assessment criteria
4.4 Explain how to recognise when a customer is angry or confused
4.5 Identify their organisation's standards for timeliness in responding to customer questions and requests for information

TUTORIAL 2 with your virtual advisor:

Read through this tutorial so that you can meet the requirements of the assessment criteria shown above.

4.4 Explain how to recognise when a customer is angry or confused

Before you can recognise when a customer is angry or confused you need to understand and recognise what they want and need from you. (We have already discussed this in Chapter 1 Unit F1.) You also need to have a basic understanding of human behaviour and be able to identify emotions in yourself and others. This is known as emotional intelligence; in simple terms this is the ability to recognise your own emotions and how this can impact on your relationship with others and to be able to recognise the emotions of others and the triggers that can affect them.

Much of our communication takes place at a sub-conscious level and depends on our body language or tone of voice. When we interact with a person we have a basic instinct which helps us decide what and how they are trying to communicate with us. We all have our own history, shaped by how we are treated by others, especially our parents, partners and children, and this affects our ability to communicate. Your customer's current state of happiness and personal circumstances will also affect their communication as well. Although there is no way you can identify all this from a short transaction, you can look for clues.

Angry or confused customers will often communicate in different 'transactional states':

- like a child – shouting, demanding, sulky, hard-done by
- like a parent – controlling, critical, complaining, condescending
- like an adult – logical, factual, efficient, organised.

As a customer service professional, you need to recognise the customer's transactional state, particularly when a customer is angry or confused. You need to be aware that if your customer is in the negative state of parent or child it will not help the situation to mirror this. It is often better to behave like a positive adult and be logical, factual and professional, with a degree of 'nurturing parent' showing understanding and care.

Emotional intelligence and transactional analysis are relevant topics for a customer service professional to research as they provide a deeper insight into the behaviour of customers. There is a wealth of information on the internet to signpost you to further reading.

Figure A4.4

Let us now look at some of the reasons why customers become angry or confused.

- The method of communication selected was not suitable.
- The message or information was not clear.
- There was little empathy from the customer service professional.
- Expectations were not met, either by a person, process or product.
- There was a lack of understanding of the customer promise.

When a customer wishes to access a service or purchase a product they will either want information to help them make an informed choice or they will have carried out some research prior to the transaction. They might have looked at the customer promise or the terms and conditions of the contract and they will have certain expectations. The customer might have booked something online, thinking it would be easier, but then found the system or process created problems. If the customer's expectations are not met (whether they are realistic or not), they will become confused or angry. If you are unable to explain why their expectations cannot be met or provide a compromise this will compound their anger or confusion.

Let us consider again what happened in Case study 1. Liz failed to recognise that the customer was looking forward to and excited about making a purchase at what she thought was a bargain price. She also did not identify that the customer was confused about the organisation's policy and her statutory rights and then became disappointed and angry because her expectations were not met. Liz compounded this by letting her own emotions affect her behaviour and by not actively listening and watching for clues in the customer's behaviour. Liz also failed to clarify the legal position on returns; if she had been able to say that the customer's statutory rights were unaffected she might have saved the sale. Instead, the outcome was a disappointed and humiliated customer who left the shop, probably never to return.

Now let us think about the customer's perspective: she may have overreacted but this was due to how Liz made her feel at the time – Liz failed to care for her emotions. It is the responsibility of the customer service professional to adapt the way they deal with the customer according to the customer's emotions and to try to find a way to help them come to terms with the result.

Questions

1. Over the last month how have you allowed your emotions to get in the way of customer service delivery? How did you do this and what was the outcome?

2. Analyse two interactions with your customers during the past week. During these transactions what emotional state was your customer in?

3. How did you adapt your transactional state to deal with your customer?

4.5 Identify their organisation's standards for timeliness in responding to customer questions and requests for information

We have already mentioned in previous chapters that most customer-focused organisations have in place a set of customer service guidelines or minimum standards. Some of the standards are based on the standards for timeliness in responding to customer questions and requests for information and may be very simple: for example, your customer might be expecting to be assisted within a certain time frame, such as a response to an enquiry within 24 hours, the telephone to be answered within four rings, or an order to arrive within three working days. It is important that you know and understand your organisation's standards and that you meet them. Often customer service professionals are assessed against their organisation's standards and there will be an audit to check that they are being met. Here are some examples of standards.

- A company headquarters requires all branches to email the weekly sales figures by 12 noon on a Monday.

- Local council's customer charter: Letters, faxes and emails: 'our aim is to provide an answer within 5 working days'. Telephone: 'our aim is to answer the phone within 20 seconds'.

- A well-known bank complaints promise published on its website: '… Accordingly, we have in place a 24-hour Contact Centre to attend to your enquiries and a dedicated unit to look into all complaints and we endeavour to resolve your complaint as promptly as possible. In any event, our policy necessitates us to revert to you within 2 business days from the day of receipt of your complaint.'

- A large retailer encourages their customer service professionals to make contact as soon as customers come into the store by saying they are here to help and stating their name. This is followed up by a check at the point of sale by another member of staff asking if someone has helped them during their visit. Often there will be a mystery shopper test to check if the standards of timeliness have been met.

It is important that you know and understand the standards for timeliness in responding to your internal and external customers. The standards are usually there for a reason and others may be depending on you to enable them to carry out their role.

Questions

1. List the standards for timeliness in responding to customers' questions and requests in your own organisation.

2. Find out the same information for two organisations in the same sector.

3. How do these standards compare to the standards in your organisation?

The reflective activity below is designed to start you thinking about your reactions and feelings when you have encountered different customer service scenarios. The activity is from the perspective of you as the customer. We are all customers on a regular basis and this activity will help to prepare you to collect evidence that will demonstrate your knowledge, understanding and practical skills in customer service. You can write down your reflections if you wish as you may find them useful in discussions or questioning sessions with your assessor or in the preparation of your evidence.

Think about a scenario when you were the customer and you experienced a customer service professional communicating in a very positive manner.

1. Reflect on the method of communication they used and how appropriate it was for your needs.
2. Why was it a positive experience?
3. How did the customer service professional engage on an emotional level with you and what transactional state were you both in?

Now think of a time when you experienced a less than satisfactory situation and you were angry or confused.

1. Was it the customer service professional's behaviour, timeliness or knowledge that caused the anger or confusion?
2. How did they deal with your emotions?
3. How did the customer service professional's subsequent behaviour, timeliness or knowledge affect the situation?

If you cannot think of any examples then ask a colleague, family member or friend about their experiences.

Performance evidence for Unit A4 (LO1, LO2, LO3)

So far the case study has given you the opportunity to consider the customer service provided by Liz and the impact this had on her customer. The reflective activities have enabled you to look at the methods of communication you use to communicate with your customers, as well as the customer service experience that you have received from others.

The next section in this unit is designed to help you focus on the learning outcomes and performance requirement of Unit A4 and prompt you to think how you can evidence it through your customer service role. It is expected that the evidence that you generate for this unit will also cross-reference with some of the optional units that you have selected. The virtual advisor will guide you to collect the evidence that you need to complete this unit.

Performance evidence is different from knowledge evidence and requires you to identify events that have happened in the course of your job in a real work environment. You will have to prove that the customers really exist and the events or incidents really happened – your assessor will help you to do this. The ways that you can present the evidence will be explained in Tutorial 3 below. You should answer the questions in the context of where you work and your provision of customer service. This time it *is* important for you to record your answers in writing as this will be the foundation of your evidence. However, you need only write notes to remind you where the proof is located.

LO1 Establish rapport with customers

Assessment criteria

1.1 Meet their organisation's standards of appearance and behaviour
1.2 Greet their customer respectfully and in a friendly manner
1.3 Communicate with their customer in a way that makes them feel valued and respected
1.4 Identify and confirm their customer's expectations
1.5 Treat their customer courteously and helpfully at all times
1.6 Keep their customer informed and reassured
1.7 Adapt their behaviour to respond to different customer behaviour

LO2 Responding appropriately to customers

Assessment criteria

2.1 Respond promptly to a customer seeking help
2.2 Choose the most appropriate way to communicate with their customer
2.3 Check with their customer that they have fully understood their expectations
2.4 Respond promptly and positively to their customer's questions and comments
2.5 Allow their customer time to consider their response and give further explanation when appropriate

TUTORIAL 3 with your virtual advisor:

The knowledge supporting the assessment criteria for learning outcomes 1 and 2 (see above) has been discussed in learning outcome 4 earlier in this chapter. You were asked to provide some examples of how you meet the requirements of the standards in your organisation, the methods of communication that you use with your customers and how you respond to different types of customer behaviour. You also considered the importance of timeliness in responding to customer requests, providing more information to the customer to ensure their understanding and the importance of emotional intelligence when dealing with customers.

The evidence you need to produce for this unit could be an observation by your assessor of you working and interacting with your customers and colleagues. Observation with some questioning could capture all seven criteria of LO1 and all five criteria of LO5. Use the ideas or notes that you have already made for learning outcome 4 to prepare for a professional discussion or a personal statement/case study (verbal or written) with your assessor. Evidence will need to be supported by work products such as the letters and emails you receive, documentation you complete for customers or witness statements from your manager or colleagues. The evidence that you present should cover as many of the assessment criteria for this unit as possible and cross-reference to some of your optional units.

In some cases you will not be able to include work product evidence because of confidentiality or data protection regulations. In this instance you can ask your manager or a colleague to confirm that you establish rapport with customers.

Evidence requirements provide the context in which you meet the assessment criteria for performance and will enable your assessor to judge whether you are competent in a number of different situations. You do not need to cover the evidence requirements separately; they will be covered as you complete the assessment criteria. Your assessor will give you guidance. The evidence requirements for Unit A4 are explained in Tutorial 5 below.

Performance evidence activity 1

Write down or make notes for use in a discussion or personal statement your answers to the questions below.

1. Within your area of responsibility what are your standards of appearance and how do you know you are maintaining them?

2. What are your workplace standards of behaviour and who confirms you are maintaining them?

3. Provide some examples of some phrases that you use to greet your customers. What proof or feedback do you have from colleagues that you treat your customers respectfully and in a friendly manner?

Look for some examples of work products, such as an email or feedback from your customer to provide evidence of the above. Ask a witness to confirm you consistently maintain the standards identified above.

LO3 Communicate information to customers

Assessment criteria

3.1 Quickly find information that will help their customer
3.2 Give their customer information they need about the services or products offered by their organisation
3.3 Recognise information that their customer might find complicated and check whether they fully understand
3.4 Explain clearly to their customers any reasons why their expectations cannot be met

TUTORIAL 4 with your virtual advisor:

To achieve the assessment criteria in this learning outcome you need to pull together all of your knowledge of the products and services you offer, your organisation's procedures and your communication skills. Preparation for dealing with your customers is important at the start of every shift or transaction. This means having all the information available or knowing where to locate it as well as who can help you. The speed with which you access the information and respond to the customer will be linked to the service promise or agreements that have been made.

In stage 4 of the cycle of effective communication and Tutorial 2 you looked at the need to pick up clues from your customer's reactions, through verbal and body language as well as voice tone and comments. This will provide an indication of whether they have understood the information you are providing and whether further explanation is required. In Chapter 2 Unit F2 (assessment criterion 2.2) and Chapter 7 Unit C1 (assessment criterion 3.2) we examine the need to understand the limits of what you are able to do for your customer. It is important that you are able to communicate this information in a way that the customer understands and will accept. Positive verbal or body language and confidence that what you are saying or doing is based on factual information will help to convey the message in the correct way. This is why it is essential that your knowledge of products and services is up to date and you know who to speak to if you need to confirm the accuracy of information.

The best way to evidence the assessment criteria in learning outcome 3 will be through observation. Alternatively, you and your assessor might consider a professional discussion or personal statement supported by work products such as emails and letters or witness statements from colleagues or your supervisor.

Performance evidence activity 2

Write down or make notes for use in a discussion your answers to the questions below.

1. Describe a transaction when you were not able to meet your customer's expectations. How did you communicate this to them?

2. Identify a transaction when you realised that the customer was finding the information complicated. How did you simplify it for them to promote understanding?

TUTORIAL 5 with your virtual advisor:

In order to cover the evidence requirements you must provide evidence of following the rules to deliver customer service.

- *Your communication with customers may be face-to-face, in writing, by telephone, text message, email, internet (including social networking), intranet or by any other method you would be expected to use within your job role.* This evidence requirement is self-explanatory and indicates the different ways that you might communicate with your customers. It is very flexible; the reference to 'other methods' could cover communication methods that are specialist to your organisation. You will need to explain in detail if the method you use is not one of the conventional methods listed above.

- *You must provide evidence of creating a positive impression with customers during routine delivery of customer service.* This is when you are working in normal circumstances, i.e. not under extra pressure or dealing with unusual circumstances like holiday periods or seasonal surges (national holidays). You will need to establish what is normal!

- *You must provide evidence of creating a positive impression with customers during a busy time in your job.* Once you have decided on the routine delivery of customer service, you will be able to identify your busy times. Quite often you will be aware of the times when you are busy and can take this into consideration when selecting opportunities for your evidence collection.

- *You must provide evidence of creating a positive impression with customers during a quiet time in your job.* In the same way you have identified a busy time in your job, you should also be able to identify quiet times. Do you find things to do or do you sit around looking bored? Think about the impression your behaviour gives to the customer. A proactive customer service professional will be able to provide a more individual service to customers when things are quiet. Think about the activities that you carry out when there is some downtime. Perhaps this is the time that you catch up on paperwork, cleaning and maintenance or carry out development activities. A busy person can look more professional; however, remember that when you do have a customer you will need to provide a positive impression of yourself and not view them as an intrusion on the activity you are undertaking.

- *You must provide evidence of creating a positive impression with customers when people, systems or resources have let you down.* Often we are unaware that other people in the customer service chain have let us down until a customer tells us that things have gone wrong. For example, a customer might telephone your organisation and have to wait in a queue for an unreasonable length of time. It will not be until they finally get through to you that you will be made aware of the problem. This is the kind of circumstance that you are likely to encounter that will meet this evidence requirement. Do you get anxious or stressed or even a bit abrupt with the customer when things go wrong? You need to provide evidence of how you create a positive impression under difficult circumstances, how you demonstrate calm and business-like behaviour, and how you avoid transferring your annoyance or irritation to the customer. Remember the transactional states that you and your customers can be in. These states are affected by other people or by inanimate objects like your computer.

A further part of the evidence requirements of this unit is the need to demonstrate that you communicate with customers effectively in a number of different ways.

- *You must provide evidence that you communicate with customers effectively by using appropriate spoken or written language.* Tutorial 1, assessment criterion 4.3 and Reflective activity 1 earlier in the chapter asked you to look at the most appropriate methods of communication for use with your customers in your area of responsibility. You need to draw on your knowledge of what is acceptable and use this to support your evidence. If you have been able to provide witness statements or written feedback from the earlier activity and have discussed this with your tutor or assessor this will support this evidence requirement.

  You also need to prove that you use the most appropriate spoken or written language when you deal with your customers. The best way to do this is observation by your assessor or by getting feedback from your manager, supervisor, colleagues or your customer. This should support any discussions or personal statements that you have made.

- *You must provide evidence that you communicate with customers effectively by applying the conventions and rules appropriate to the method of communication you have chosen.* You might already have carried out some research to examine the conventions (standards) and rules that apply to each method of communication you use in your organisation. If not, there are a number of books available online or in the library that can assist you with the conventions of written communication. for example, *Eats Shoots and Leaves: The Zero Tolerance Approach to Punctuation* by Lynne Truss.
  Certain conventions apply when sending emails:
  - You can be less formal than a letter, so you do not have to use 'dear'.
  - If you are sending attachments you should mention it in the email.
  - When you close the email you can use phrases like: regards, kind regards, best wishes.
  - You will need to include a signature: this might be your full name, title and the organisation name and address.
  - You should not use uppercase words in emails as this could be interpreted as shouting or anger.

If you are using text in communications with your customers you need to establish whether or not abbreviations are acceptable. However, the most important factor is that you find out what is acceptable in your organisation and ensure that you comply with this.

The information that you will gather from Performance activity 5 and feedback from your manager or supervisor (in a one-to-one meeting or following a quality check) will be useful in a discussion with your assessor and will support any personal statements or observations that you use in your portfolio.

Performance evidence activity 3

Analyse and make notes about a positive customer service transaction (face-to-face, email, letter, text, internet or intranet) during a busy time in your job, a quiet time in your job or during routine delivery of customer service where you think you have:

- communicated with your customer in a way that made them feel valued and respected
- identified and confirmed your customers' needs and expectations. Think about the way you tried to plan and assess what those needs and expectations were
- ensured that you treated your customer in a polite and helpful manner throughout the transaction
- checked that the comments you made to your customer to keep them informed and reassured had the intended effect.

1. How do you know whether you used the most appropriate method of communication?
2. Did anybody witness this transaction?
3. Did you ask for, or receive feedback, to confirm this transaction?

Pull all of this information together so that you can explain the transaction in detail and justify your actions and behaviour to your assessor.

Performance evidence activity 4

Provide an example of a recent customer service transaction when people, systems or resources have let you down and it affected the service that you provided to the customer.

- What was the scenario?
- What caused the transaction to go wrong?
- Were there any points at which there was a danger of you or others reacting in a negative manner?
- How did you rescue the situation?
- How would you avoid this happening again?

1. Did anybody witness this transaction?
2. Did you ask for, or receive feedback, to confirm this transaction?

Pull all of this information together so that you can explain the transaction in detail and justify your actions and behaviour to your assessor.

Performance evidence activity 5

1. What are the rules and conventions (i.e. practice or standards) for the most frequently used methods of communication (verbal, written or non-verbal) in your organisation?

2. How is your standard of practice measured against the rules and conventions?

If you cannot find any rules or standards within your organisation then look for some information on the internet, bookshop or library that might give you a few tips or insight into the rules that are adopted by businesses. Once you have found this out you may want to discuss them in a team meeting or a one-to-one with your manager. This will be a way of raising the standards of communication within your organisation and will show that you are a proactive customer service professional.

Pull all of this information together so that you can explain how you met the rules and conventions in Performance activities 3 and 4.

LEARNER EVALUATION ACTIVITY

The last activity is the learner evaluation. Each section in this chapter is intended to help you to develop yourself towards being a more thinking and reflective customer service professional. The learner evaluation requires you to reflect on your learning from completing this unit guide. Once again, this does not have to be written; however, it could be very useful to record your answers for use in reviews with your line manager, supervisor, assessor or tutor or possibly in a job interview.

Documenting your learning throughout your working life is a very effective way of showing that you use experience to influence your performance and behaviours. Reflect on what you knew at the start of the unit and what you know now.

1. What have you learned from completing this unit?

2. Identify communication facts that were new to you.

3. How will completing this unit affect your customer service within your organisation?

4. Highlight an improvement that you have made as a result of completing the unit.

If you are working towards Unit D3 Develop personal performance through delivering customer service, your evaluations might provide you with some foundation evidence.

Summary

This concludes the unit guidance for A4 Give customers a positive impression of yourself and your organisation.

You should be prepared to submit evidence for both the knowledge and performance aspects of the unit learning outcomes:

LO1: Establish rapport with customers
LO2: Respond appropriately to customers
LO3: Communicate information to customers
LO4: Understand how to give customers a positive impression of themselves and the organisation

You will now be able to describe how your customer service role fits into the organisation and the standards of appearance and behaviour that you are expected to demonstrate.

It is likely that the knowledge and performance evidence you produce for this unit will cross reference to the following Customer Service units:

- Unit A10 Dealing with customers face to face
- Unit A11 Deal with incoming telephone calls from customers
- Unit B2 Deliver reliable customer service
- Unit C1 Recognise and deal with customer queries requests and problems
- Unit D1 Develop customer relationships
- Unit F1 Communicate using customer service language

DEAL WITH CUSTOMERS FACE TO FACE

Learning outcomes

Learning outcomes for Unit A10:

1. Communicate effectively with their customer
2. Improve the rapport with their customer through body language
3. Understand how to deal with customers face to face

Introduction

This unit guide is a resource to help you gather the evidence that you require to achieve Unit A10, one of the optional units in the 'Impression and image' theme of the Level 2 NVQ Certificate in Customer Service. It can be used as a learning resource if you are new to your role, are studying customer service in preparation for work or as a refresher if you are an experienced customer service professional.

Deal with customers face to face – what is Unit A10 about?

This unit requires you to demonstrate how you communicate effectively with your customers and improve your rapport with customers through your body language.
  Unit A10 is about:

'... the skills you need to deal with your customer in person and face to face. When you are working with a customer in this way, good feelings about the way you look and behave can improve how your customer feels about the transaction and give them greater satisfaction. Whilst verbal communication is important, your focus on your customer and the relationship that is formed also depends on the non-verbal communication that takes place between you. You will have many opportunities to impress your customer and your behaviour in this situation can make all the difference to customer behaviour and the satisfaction that they feel.

Source: Adapted from Unit A10 purpose and aim

You will be required to show that you understand how to deal with customers face to face and can explain how to use a range of communication and listening techniques and non-verbal signs including body language. This includes being able to understand the difference between assertive, aggressive and passive behaviour and being able to explain different customer expectations and requirements.

Completing this unit guide

To complete this unit guide you will need to:

1. Read through the information in each section.
2. Look at the case study and reflective activity and use the questions to help you to test your understanding.

There is no set format for working through or recording your answers in these sections, just use them in a way that suits your learning style, unless otherwise instructed by your assessor or tutor. The case study and reflective activity are linked to the assessment criteria in learning outcome 3, which focuses on the underpinning knowledge and understanding for Unit A10. Learning outcome 3 has been presented first so that you understand the background to the criteria in learning outcomes 1 and 2. If you work through this section first you will find that your performance evidence will be easier to identify and present to your assessor.

Learning outcome 3 – Knowledge evidence

LO3 Understand how to deal with customers face to face

- The tutorial section is designed to explain the assessment criteria. In this section your virtual advisor will provide you with information to help you interpret the national standards.
- The case study and reflective activity will help you to prepare to discuss and explain your understanding of customer service with your assessor.

Learning outcomes 1 and 2 – Performance evidence

LO1 Communicate effectively with their customer
LO2 Improve the rapport with their customer through body language

In addition to the learning outcomes in this unit, there are performance **evidence requirements** that indicate the circumstances or conditions under which you should present the evidence.

Your evidence must include examples of dealing with customers who:

- have standard expectations of your organisation's customer service
- have experienced difficulties when dealing with your organisation
- have made a specific request for information
- need to be informed of circumstances of which they are unaware.

Your evidence must include examples of dealings with customers that are:

- planned
- unplanned.

You must provide evidence of dealing with customers face to face:

- during routine delivery of customer service
- during a busy time in your job
- during a quiet time in your job
- when people, systems or resources have let you down.

You must include examples of how you have made use of:

- verbal communication skills
- non-verbal communication skills.

In all three learning outcomes the performance evidence activities, assisted by your virtual assessor, will help you reflect on your performance and knowledge as a customer service professional. The performance evidence activities will also help you to identify and gather evidence.

The evidence requirements shown above highlight the range of circumstances and examples that you need to demonstrate in learning outcomes 1 and 2.

Why do I need to provide effective face-to-face communication to my customers?

Customer service underpins everything you do in your work role. If you are involved in providing products or services to others, whether internal or external to your organisation, it is essential that you are able to:

- converse with your customer
- demonstrate effective listening skills
- explain the services and products offered by your organisation
- balance and manage the demands of a number of customers
- constantly seek to improve rapport with your customer through effective body language.

The cycle of effective face-to-face communication

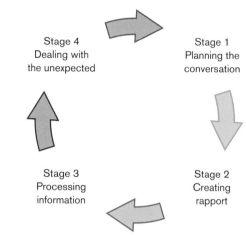

Figure A10.1: The cycle of effective face-to-face communication

We begin with some background information about the essentials of effective face-to-face communication.

The cycle of effective face-to-face communication illustrates four important stages of a customer service transaction. In Chapter 3 Unit A4 we looked at the cycle of effective communication; however, this was not specific to any one method. In this chapter we will look at face-to-face interaction with your customer, whether they are internal (colleagues, managers, service partners) or external to your organisation.

Stage 1 Planning the conversation

When you plan a conversation with a customer it is vital you decide what you are going to say. Prior to any face-to-face transaction you will have a general idea of the needs and requirements of the customer that you are about to speak to. For example, if you work in a retail setting you will know that your customers will ask you questions about your products and services. If you work in an office environment you will know who are your internal and external customers and the general questions and queries that you are likely to be faced with. In all situations you need to be prepared for your conversation – you should prepare greetings and relevant information and anticipate questions. This might be a set of phrases that you have been told to use or information about products that you have sourced from the internet, colleagues or suppliers. As discussed in Chapter 3, preparation is essential – failing to prepare is preparing to fail.

Stage 2 Creating rapport

Stage 2 in the cycle of effective face-to-face communication concentrates on establishing a rapport. Rapport is a positive chemistry between you and the customer by finding and sharing common values, beliefs, knowledge or behaviours.

In Chapter 3 Unit A4 we discussed expected standards of appearance and behaviour. When you are communicating face to face you need to be sure that you are conforming to the expectations of your organisation and your customer. This includes the messages you send out to your customer: the way you dress, the verbal language you use and the body language that you convey.

It is not just the messages that you give out that are important but also the messages your customer is providing to you, and how you interpret them. This means careful, active and empathetic listening and looking for signals and clues from your customer.

Stage 3 Processing information

Once you have planned the conversation, created rapport and listened to your customer it is important to process the information correctly. Once again, your listening skills are vital so that you do not overlay your own values and beliefs about the customer and their needs and you hear what is really being said. It is also about knowing your products and services and being able to match these to your customers.

Stage 4 Dealing with the unexpected

No matter how well you have planned the conversation, created rapport, listened to and observed your customer and processed the information, things can get complicated in the cycle of communication. During a transaction there can be interference from the environment and other people. This can be in the form of noise, interruptions, conflicting information or differing opinions. It is vital that you have an understanding of how to balance the needs of the customer and what is going on around you. You may be dealing with multiple enquiries and demanding customers. You will need a strategy of how to keep calm and manage the situation without losing your rapport with the customer.

Knowledge evidence for Unit A10 (LO3)

As stated earlier, we will begin with learning outcome 3 (LO3). This contains the knowledge criteria for the unit and it is essential that you have the knowledge to underpin your performance.

LO3 Understand how to deal with customers face to face

F1.3 Assessment criteria

3.1 Explain the importance of speaking clearly and slowly when dealing with a customer face to face
3.2 State the importance of taking the time to listen carefully to what the customer is saying
3.3 Identify the organisation's procedures that impact on the way they are able to deal with their customers face to face
3.4 Describe the features and benefits of the organisation's services or products.

TUTORIAL 1 with your virtual advisor:

Read through this tutorial so that you can meet the requirements of the assessment criteria shown above.

3.1 Explain the importance of speaking clearly and slowly when dealing with a customer face to face

In the course of a day we speak to many people and often the interaction will be face to face. Depending on where you work, you will have to deal with a variety of customers, all of whom will have different communication needs. These needs could be linked to their age, language needs, culture and their prior knowledge of products or services. All of this must be taken into consideration when you plan your conversation and make an assessment of the customer; often your assessment of their needs will be carried out in the space of a few seconds.

When you evidence this assessment criterion you will need to bear the following in mind:

- You will need to explain the importance of speaking slowly and clearly in the context of the customers that you deal with.

- When you speak to your customers you must take their needs into consideration and adapt your speech accordingly. This means being clear and precise about what you want to say and thinking about the tone and pitch of your voice. For example, when dealing with a more mature customer do not assume that you have to talk loudly and remember not to mumble.

- It is always best to have eye contact with the customer and face them so that they can see your mouth as this will help them to process what you are saying. However, do not crowd or intimidate them with your physical presence.

- Consider the timing and the speed of what you are saying; in the same way as talking loudly or too softly can impair the message so can speaking too quickly or slowly.

In conclusion, it is important to speak clearly and slowly so that the message is conveyed to the customer with the least misunderstanding or interference possible.

Questions

1. List three different types of customer that you come into contact with face to face.

2. How do you adjust the way you speak to each of them according to their characteristics and needs?

3. Why is it important to adjust the pace and clarity of your speech with each of these customers?

3.2 State the importance of taking the time to listen carefully to what the customer is saying

We have already mentioned in previous chapters, the importance of good listening skills. This may be active listening where you pay attention to words, body language and facial expressions, but also empathetic listening where you are:

- paying full attention to what your customer is saying – tone and pace of their speech, emphasis, facial expressions
- showing an awareness of cultural or ethnic values and beliefs
- feeling through your senses (visual, auditory, smell), often on a subconscious level
- showing empathy through gestures and posture, nodding or smiling from time to time to show that you are interested and engaged in the conversation
- giving your full attention and not being distracted by what is going on around you
- watching your customer's body language, looking for clues that they might be relaxed, agitated, confused or angry
- allowing your customer to complete their sentences or conversations without interruption. Butting in before they finish demonstrates that you are more interested in your own point of view than theirs
- receiving feedback by checking that you have understood what they are saying.

When evidencing this assessment criterion it is important that you can provide examples to your assessor of your experiences with customers and explain why it was so important to listen to them.

Questions

1. Ask a colleague, supervisor or manager to observe you and assess whether you put all the above points into practice.
2. Ask them to indicate one area that you could improve upon. If you have been assessed through an organisation quality check then you could use this as evidence.

3.3 Identify the organisation's procedures that impact on the way they are able to deal with their customers face to face

When dealing with customers face to face you need to be aware of some of the organisation procedures that might impact on the transaction. For example, a customer service professional working in a bank may not be able to meet with their customers away from their desk because of security needs. They will therefore have to convey a friendly and professional image from behind the counter. It may be difficult at times for them to speak to their customers in confidence, so they will have to think about the language, tone and volume of their conversation. They might be constrained by organisation procedures relating to data protection and confidentiality as well as the security of the money they are handling. This could result in explaining to their customers that some of the information can only be provided in a written format. The procedures that have a bearing on your face-to-face service will vary but you need to think about them so that you can explain them to your assessor.

Question

1. Identify at least one procedure that impacts on how you deal with a customer face to face in your organisation. If you cannot think of one then talk to your manager or a friend or colleague in a customer service role outside your organisation.

3.4 Describe the features and benefits of the organisation's services or products

We discussed the features and benefits of an organisation's services or products in Chapter 1, Tutorial 2. You were asked to reflect on your own organisation's products and services and it was pointed out that you are able to obtain this information from a number of sources:

- your manager/supervisor and colleagues
- the training that you had when you started your job
- ongoing training
- through team meetings and communication sessions
- your customer promise
- brochures and advertisements
- the internet
- your suppliers and manufacturers.

You need to be aware not only of the products and services offered within your own department/area/branch/office but also who supports and complements you and what they can offer.

Once you have a sound understanding of your products and services you should be able to identify and explain the features and benefits of each to your customers. However, before you can do this you need to know the following.

What is a feature?

A feature is a point that describes what a product or service can do for the customer. An everyday example is an electric kettle – its features might include:

- capacity
- colour
- speed of water boil
- environmental factors, i.e. how much electricity it uses per boil
- a limescale filter.

What is a benefit?

Every feature has a potential benefit for a customer, but a benefit to one customer might not be to another. For example:

- The benefit of a coloured kettle is that you can match it to your kitchen colour scheme and other appliances.

- A 1.5 litre capacity might be a benefit to a family of four, but not to a person living on their own.
- A limescale filter might be helpful if you live in a hard water area but not necessary if you live in an area with soft water.

As a customer service professional you need to look at all your products and services and decide what features and benefits might appeal to your typical customers. This is an activity best undertaken with colleagues so that you can all agree and standardise your approach. Be aware that one size does not fit all! If you have already done this exercise for Unit F1 then you might be able to use this evidence again.

Question

1. Identify two of your main services or products and then explain the features and the benefits that might apply to the customers you identified in the questions for assessment criteria 3.1.

The case study provides an opportunity for you to read about a scenario and consolidates some of the information from the tutorial. You can use this to reflect on the situation and answer some questions. Again, you do not have to write your answers down unless your tutor or assessor has asked you to do so.

CASE STUDY 1 The new shower

Mr Jones is 95 years old. He lives on his own and manages his house with the help of his carer. Mr Jones was finding it difficult to get in and out of the bath and decided that he wanted a shower to replace the bath.

Mr Jones and his carer visited a well-known bath retailer. Joe, the salesperson, was very knowledgeable about the products and service offered and was able to explain the types of shower that would fit best in the customer's bathroom. He assessed Mr Jones' needs by asking questions and observing his movement and body language. He demonstrated products to confirm their suitability for Mr Jones and he explained, from a safety perspective, that Mr Jones needed to have the shower panels fixed with ceiling brackets. He recommended taps that would be easy to use because he could see Mr Jones had swollen finger joints. He explained that the bathroom suite came in different heights and recommended the one that would be best for the customer as he had picked up from a comment Mr Jones made that he had painful knee joints. Joe also took the measurements of the bathroom and produced a plan of the layout for Mr Jones. He had a list of bathroom fitters who would be able to carry out the work and he suggested that Mr Jones and his carer checked out all of the fitters on 'Check-a-builder', an online service that rates the quality of workmanship.

Mr Jones and his carer settled on Bill Wyatt, who had very good ratings for workmanship on Check-a-builder. Bill came along to Mr Jones' house and met with him. On first glance, Bill noticed Mr Jones was wearing a hearing aid. They went in to the bathroom and Bill got down on his knees to look under the bath. He started to speak to Mr Jones who did not hear what he said, so Bill raised his voice and started shouting. Mr Jones still did not respond and Bill started to get annoyed. Bill's mobile telephone went off and he spent ten minutes sitting on the bathroom floor having an argument with a supplier. Mr Jones found standing for a long period difficult so he went out and sat in his study while he waited for Bill to finish. When he at last finished his call, Bill looked at the fittings and fixtures that Mr Jones had purchased and started to lecture Mr Jones about how he could not install some of them in the bathroom. His tone was very patronising and bossy. Mr Jones' carer started to explain the reasoning behind the purchases and the advice and help they were given by the bathroom retailer. Bill made a comment about the salesman not knowing what he was talking about. He then turned his back on her and started to talk to Mr Jones about changing the shower fittings.

Mr Jones and his carer were both taken aback by his attitude and manner. However, they wanted to get the bathroom completed as soon as possible to avoid Mr Jones having an accident. Before Bill left they arranged to cancel their order for the shower and purchase a more expensive one from a supplier recommended by Bill. He gave them a date that he would start the work.

Two days before the work was due to commence the carer was very worried that she had not heard anything from Bill and the new fixtures and fittings had not arrived, so she decided to telephone him. When she got through to him she put him on speaker phone so Mr Jones could hear. Bill told her that he had not promised to start on that date, that they must have misunderstood him and that he would not be able to carry out the work until he returned from holiday in a month, and then it might be a couple of weeks after that.

When the carer tried to establish the misunderstanding and highlighted the safety need for the new bathroom, Bill called around in person to talk to Mr Jones and the carer. He responded in a defensive and aggressive manner and moved so close to Mr Jones in the confined space of the bathroom that Mr Jones was forced out of the door and nearly fell over.

The carer and Mr Jones were very upset by the interaction and they decided not to use Bill to install the bathroom. They could not complain on Check-a-builder about Bill's work because he had not carried out any work for them; however, they went into the bathroom retailer to complain about his attitude and integrity and to ask them to remove him from their recommended list of installers. Joe, seeing Mr Jones' distress, telephoned a bathroom fitter that he had personally used and arranged for him to do the work the following week.

Questions

1. How did the bathroom retailer demonstrate that he recognised Mr Jones' needs?

2. What did Bill do wrong during the face-to-face interaction with Mr Jones and his carer?

3. How could Bill have improved his face-to-face communication skills during his meeting?

LO3 Understand how to deal with customers face to face

Assessment criteria

3.5 Explain the organisation's service offer and how it affects the way they deal with customers face to face

3.6 Explain the principles of body language that enables them to interpret customer feelings without verbal communication

3.7 Explain the difference between behaving assertively, aggressively and passively

3.8 Explain why the expectations and behaviour of individual customers will demand different responses to create rapport and achieve customer satisfaction

3.9 Describe the agreed and recognised signs in customer behaviour in their organisation that indicates their customer expects a particular action by them.

TUTORIAL 2 with your virtual advisor:

Read through this tutorial so that you can meet the requirements of the assessment criteria shown above.

3.5 Explain the organisation's service offer and how it affects the way they deal with customers face to face

In Chapter 1 Unit F1 assessment criteria 3.6 we looked at the definition of a service offer: 'A service offer defines the extent and limits of the customer service that an organisation is offering ...'

This can be anything that lists or states the standards of service that your customers can expect from you. A service offer can also be known as a service level agreement and is often measured by targets, for example, answering the telephone within 15 seconds, the number of calls answered in a day or the promises that your organisation advertises on the internet such as guaranteed delivery in 3 to 4 days. In summary it is what the organisation promises to do for their customers, both internal and external.

How can the service offer affect the way you deal with a customer face to face? Your service offers could include the need to greet a customer within a minute of their entering the shop and the need to answer the telephone within six rings. However, if you are working alone and the telephone rings and at the same time a customer enters the shop, you will need to decide how to prioritise the two customers. The decision will have to be made instantly, taking into consideration such things as the customer's body language – are they browsing or purposeful? What you say and do will depend on your assessment of the situation. You might decide you need to answer the telephone but you first let your shop customer know that you will be back to help them as soon as possible. You might ask the customer whether they need help or information and then excuse yourself. The call can be answered but you might have to tell the telephone customer you will ring back in a few minutes before returning to your face-to-face transaction. You must ensure you make the correct decision for the situation, that your tone, manner and facial expressions are appropriate and that you at least make eye contact and acknowledge your customer.

Questions

1. Identify a service offer that relates to face-to-face communication in your organisation.

2. How does this service offer affect how you deal with customers face to face?

3.6 Explain the principles of body language that enables them to interpret customer feelings without verbal communication

We have already identified that active listening is essential to the customer service transaction. However, equally important in a face-to-face transaction is the observation of non-verbal communication or body language. Body language is the way humans convey their feelings, moods and attitudes through the state of their body:

- facial expressions
- posture
- positioning
- gestures and movements.

Facial expressions

There are six emotions conveyed by facial expressions:

1. happiness
2. sadness
3. fear
4. disgust
5. surprise
6. anger.

Within those expressions there can be many messages passed to the receiver, for example:

- A smile (happiness) – welcoming, friendly
- Smirking (disgust) – lack of respect
- Frowning (anger) – impatience

It is not possible to accurately interpret body language from a single expression and other signals need to be taken into consideration when looking at an individual. For example:

Posture

A tilt of the head with a half smile could convey interest or sympathy. Crossed arms and a frown could be seen as defensive and verging on anger. A person slouched at a table with a smirk on their face could be interpreted as disrespectful, lazy or disinterested.

Positioning of the body

A customer might stand close to the entrance of a shop, wide eyed and fidgety and appear hesitant; this could be interpreted as being shy or nervous. Sometimes we may find ourselves in conversation with somebody who physically comes too close for our comfort. Each time we take a step back they take one forward. This is commonly known as 'invading personal space'.

Figure A10.2

Gesture and movements

Gestures add to the mix of body language: if you smile, tilt your head and indicate towards something with your hand open and palm upwards this could be seen as being helpful and welcoming. If a frown is backed up by a clenched fist then this could be seen as aggressive body language, particularly if the person takes a step toward the receiver and encroaches on their personal space.

Other gestures and movements that can influence the interpretation of non-verbal communication include, for example, frequent quick glances at the clock or a door during a conversation – this could imply disinterest or waiting for someone or something better to come along. Yawning might indicate tiredness but can also be translated as boredom.

In summary, your observation of gestures, positioning, facial expressions and posture will provide you with a picture of your customer's feelings and emotions during a transaction. Take time out to observe your customers' body language and reflect on whether your interpretation is accurate. Use your observations to develop a better understanding of your customers' non-verbal communication and your reactions.

Questions

1. Over the next few days, select three customers that you have a face-to-face conversation with and identify the facial expressions, gestures and posture of each just before you start the conversation. What did this tell you about their emotions or behaviour?

2. What was your first impression and was it correct once you had completed the transaction with them?

If you cannot access three customers try this with friends or colleagues.

3.7 Explain the differences between behaving assertively, aggressively and passively

None of us know how we sound or appear to others unless we receive feedback. What might seem perfectly acceptable behaviour with family or friends could be seen as assertive, aggressive or passive to a customer or when we are the customer. Asking for feedback will help you identify when you display each of these types of behaviour and will enable you to assess yourself in different situations.

Aggressive behaviour

Aggression is an emotion that can take over when a customer has cause to complain or there is a conflict situation in the workplace. There are several definitions of aggressive behaviour, but in the context of customer service it means to act in a hostile fashion or to behave in an intense or harsh manner. You are most likely to encounter aggression when something has gone wrong and the customer wants what they see as justice or a resolution.

Aggressive body language can often be easy to spot: a determined look on the face, an angry set of the mouth or a frown, a purposeful walk and, sometimes, finger jabbing, goods being thrown down or invasion of personal space. It is usually accompanied by a raised voice or angry tone and in extreme cases abusive language and behaviour. Although you might encounter this type of behaviour from a customer, it is not acceptable, under any circumstances, for a customer service professional to behave aggressively.

Passive behaviour

What is passive behaviour? In this context it is accepting an action without any obvious objection or resistance. Your customer might be very accepting of the information they are given and could be processing and digesting the information you have provided to them. But how can you tell whether they are satisfied and are they going to tell you if they are not?

When a customer is displaying passive behaviour it might be necessary for you to check that they are happy before the transaction goes too far. There may be uncomfortable silences in the conversation; if this happens, use the pause to allow them to take in the information, but check their understanding by asking for feedback through questions.

In the case of a passive complainer they do not usually vocalise their concerns about the problem or the service they have received. However, they might go away and tell their friends or family about their perceived negative experience. You will not be aware of this because they were passive. It might not be until you, or a colleague, check if they are happy with the service they have received that they will express their feelings and then the full force of their grievance will come out.

Passive behaviour is a difficult emotion to identify facially because the anger or anxiety the customer is feeling can be masked by a smile; however, if you look more closely their lips may be tight and compressed or they may not make positive eye contact and instead appear distant or detached. There might be sighs or a shrug of the shoulders. The aggression can be contained or the smile could be covering a feeling of confusion and it is not until the person starts to speak to you that you will recognise the confusion, sarcasm or anger in their voice.

As a customer service professional it is not useful to display passive tendencies unless you are trying to deal with an angry customer and you let them vent their anger and frustration before you start speaking. In most cases it is better to display active and empathetic listening and to respond assertively.

Assertive behaviour

Assertiveness means to confidently put across a point of view without threatening the other person's rights or ignoring or excluding their opinion. Assertiveness can be a useful behaviour for a customer service professional when dealing with a stressful situation, when providing important information to a customer or attempting to diffuse a conflict situation. Assertiveness is about knowing levels of acceptability and having control over feelings, in particular anger and talking through what can be achieved in a reasoned manner. The body language that accompanies assertiveness is good posture, frequent eye contact and smiling, without grinning or appearing over confident.

Questions

1. Think back to the three customers whose body language you observed in assessment criterion 3.6. Did they display assertive, passive or aggressive behaviour during the transaction?

2. Reflect on your own responses to customers. When have you displayed assertive, passive or aggressive behaviour during a transaction? Was this appropriate?

3.8 Explain why the expectations and behaviour of individual customers will demand different responses to create rapport and achieve customer satisfaction

You need to be able to explain to your assessor or tutor how you tailor the responses that you give to each of your customers based on their behaviours and expectations. In Tutorial 1 in Chapter 1 Unit F1 you reflected on the characteristics of the typical customers that you deal with; it is those characteristics that determine your customers' expectations and behaviour.

Let us consider again the characteristics of Mr Jones in Case Study 1. We know that he is a mature customer who has some special requirements to meet his health needs. He had an expectation that a new shower instead of his bath would make his life easier and suit his mobility capabilities. He also wanted the shower fitted as quickly as possible because he was worried about having an accident. Bill, the bathroom fitter did not take account of any of Mr Jones' expectations. Bill was there to get a job done and was not going to juggle his schedule or make any allowances because this customer might have more urgent needs than others. He did not try to create a rapport with Mr Jones by thinking about how he spoke to him and the tone of voice and body language he used was totally inappropriate. Bill considers himself a builder by trade and does not see himself as a customer service professional. However, he failed to realise that his poor customer service skills have impacted on his reputation and will damage his business. Joe, the bath salesperson, went out of his way to observe the needs of his customer and to build a rapport with him. He also managed to save the sale by thinking quickly and using his contacts. The same scenario but with a young married couple would have required Joe to provide different information and Bill's behaviour and rapport might have had less impact – it all depends on the expectations of the customer.

What is rapport?

Rapport is showing a genuine interest in another person and is built on respect and understanding. To build rapport with your customer you will need to concentrate wholly on what they are saying, observe their behaviour and empathise with their expectations. This is essential for effective communication with your customer.

There are a number of techniques to help create rapport with a customer; one of these is 'matching and mirroring'. Often this happens naturally when you build a relationship with the customer and you adopt a similar body posture, gestures and vocal tone to the other person. However, you can also do this consciously to help build rapport. Take some time to observe people in conversation and see whether they are matching and mirroring. Another technique is known as 'pacing and leading' and this can be very useful when dealing with a customer who is upset or angry. This is about allowing the customer to get something 'off their chest' before you start to provide a solution. Once they have started to calm down you can begin to build a rapport with them.

Questions

1. What methods do you use to create rapport during a face-to-face transaction?

2. Thinking again about the three customers you chose in assessment criterion 3.6, how did you adjust your method of creating rapport to obtain a satisfactory outcome?

Figure A10.3

3.9 Describe the agreed and recognised signs in customer behaviour in their organisation that indicate their customer expects a particular action by them

In the same way that you looked at your customers' characteristics in Chapter 1 you also need to examine the typical behaviour of the customers that you deal with. For example, the behaviour of a customer calling the emergency services is going to be very different to a customer in a bar or a public house.

In the first situation, the customer is likely to be distressed, anxious and in some cases irrational. They will expect a quick response and reassurance that action will be taken by experienced people. The customer service professional will need to take command of the situation and may adopt assertive behaviour with the transactional state of caring parent.

In the bar or public house example, the customers are likely to be in a relaxed mood; they could also be a bit excitable or under the influence of alcohol. Their expected behaviour might be exuberant, demanding or even verging on abusive. The customer service professional will need to be assertive as they may have to deal with customers who have unreasonable expectations, for example, service of drinks outside of licensing hours or to underage drinkers. At times the customer service professional will have to explain that the customer's expectations cannot be met.

In both examples, however, the customer service professional will need to create a rapport with the customer in order to reach a satisfactory outcome. They will need to know and understand the rules of their organisation, their legal obligations and the limits of what can be tolerated in terms of language and behaviour before they call a halt to the transaction.

Question

1. Prepare some notes (maximum of one page) to help you discuss the accepted and agreed behaviours of your typical customers and what your organisation allows and expects you to provide for them.

The reflective activity below is designed to help you to start thinking about your reactions and feelings when, as a customer, you have encountered different customer service scenarios. The activity will help you to prepare evidence that will demonstrate your knowledge, understanding and practical skills in customer service. Write down your reflections if you wish as they may be useful in discussions or sessions with your assessor or in the preparation of your evidence.

REFLECTIVE ACTIVITY 1

Analyse a recent face-to-face scenario when you were the customer and the customer service professional created a good rapport with you.

Now think of a time when you felt uncomfortable about the body language or the behaviour of the customer service professional during the customer service transaction.

Questions

1. In the case of the positive experience, what did the customer service professional do to create rapport?

2. In the case of the negative experience, what was it they did that caused you to feel uncomfortable?

If you cannot think of your own scenarios, speak to a friend, colleague, or your tutor and ask them about theirs.

Performance evidence for Unit A10 (LO1 and LO2)

The tutorial questions, case study and reflective activity have given you the opportunity to consider the face-to-face customer service provided in a customer service setting and to think about behaviour and rapport from your own experiences.

The next section in this unit is designed to help you focus on the learning outcomes and performance requirements of Unit A10 and prompt you to think how you can evidence this through your customer service role. It is expected that the evidence that you generate for this unit will also cross-reference with some of the other units in the qualification. The virtual advisor will guide you to collect the evidence that you need to complete this unit.

Performance evidence is different from knowledge evidence and requires you to identify events that have happened in the course of your job in a real work environment. You will have to demonstrate that the customers exist and the events or incidents really happened – your assessor will help you to do this. The ways that you can present the evidence will be explained in Tutorial 3. You should answer the questions in the context of where you work and your provision of customer service. This time it *is* important for you to record your answers in writing as this will be the foundation of your evidence. However, you need only write notes to remind you where the proof is located.

LO1 Communicate effectively with their customer

Assessment criteria

1.1 Plan a conversation with their customer that has structure and clear direction
1.2 Hold a conversation with their customer that establishes rapport
1.3 Focus on their customer and listen carefully to ensure that they collect all possible information they need from the conversation
1.4 Explain their services or products and their organisation's service offer to their customer clearly and concisely
1.5 Adapt their communication to meet the individual needs of their customer
1.6 Anticipate their customer's requests and needs for information

TUTORIAL 3 with your virtual advisor:

This tutorial is not intended to take the place of meetings with your assessor but to offer some support and a refresher in his or her absence.

Much of the knowledge supporting the assessment criteria in this section has been discussed in LO3, where we looked at establishing rapport and listening to the customer. We recapped on the importance of your awareness of your organisation's policies and procedures and how they impact on face-to-face transactions. Having answered the questions in earlier tutorials in this chapter, you may have already gathered some examples from your own work situation, which could be expanded upon to contribute to your performance evidence.

The first six assessment criteria in LO1 ask you to demonstrate that you can communicate with your customer in a real work situation. It is important that you can show that you are able to prepare the information that you are going to present to a customer in a typical conversation. Your conversation should have a beginning, middle and end:

- Some opening phrases: an introduction to the meeting or transaction.
- The information that you wish to communicate: facts about the products and services, the features and benefits, the legal information and other relevant data.
- Closing phrases: to clinch the deal; actions for others; follow-up services, after-care, complaints procedures and an explanation of your actions.

The next stage is to hold your conversation with the customer and build a rapport with them. This will be based on some of the knowledge you have about the characteristics of your customers, their behaviours, needs and expectations. Think about practising active and empathetic listening skills, taking in the words and tone used by the individual customer, their body language and facial expressions and balancing your listening and verbal skills according to their needs.

Develop and build your skills by reflecting on and evaluating each customer meeting or transaction that you experience. Some will go well and others not in the way you anticipated. Always consider what you could have done better and use this next time. This is known as self-assessment and continuous improvement and is a sound business skill. We will look at this in more detail in Chapter 9 Unit D3.

Performance evidence activity 1

Identify a face-to-face transaction or meeting that you have or will be carrying out.

1. What do you want to say and achieve from the meeting?
2. How will you create rapport with the customer, based on their needs?
3. How will you convey the information?

Make notes of the transaction or meeting: the opening or introduction, the information to be conveyed, the questions you think the customer might ask and how you will close the transaction or meeting. Discuss these with your assessor and use the notes as the basis of a discussion or questions.

LO1 Communicate effectively with their customer

Assessment criteria

1.7 Balance conflicting demands for their attention whilst maintaining rapport with their current customer
1.8 Calm down situations when one customer is adversely affecting the customer service enjoyed by other customers.

TUTORIAL 4 with your virtual advisor:

Many customer service professionals have to deal with a number of customers at busy times or when they are short-staffed. This can cause stress for both parties and may lead to negative behaviour such as anger or aggression and complaints.

Dealing with conflicting demands is a skill that needs to be developed by having a strategy in place for when customer care becomes too much to handle. An obvious strategy is to ask your customers to form a queue and wait their turn; however, even this can cause adverse behaviour in the customer. In a number of banks customers are still asked to queue but a customer service professional will ask waiting customers about the type of transaction they wish to make and direct them to an alternative source of help to speed up the transaction. Other tactics include providing toys if your customers tend to be parents waiting with children or using an appointment or numbered ticket system at times when it is known to get busy. It will be the responsibility of your manager or supervisor to identify times when resources might be stretched, but you can contribute to this by alerting them to situations when the level of service has been affected by demand.

In situations where these tactics are not feasible it will be your responsibility to manage the expectations of your customers by alerting them to a delay or explaining calmly and assertively that you will be with them as soon as possible, and perhaps diverting their attention during the waiting time by providing a brochure or some information to read, or by asking them to return in a realistic time frame.

Your spoken language, body language and facial expressions will be vital to maintain rapport with your current customer and other customers demanding your attention. This means providing:

- a smile

- an apologetic word or phrase

- an inclusive gesture, for example, an indication where the diversion is located or where they can get water or coffee.

A further solution may be to ask your current customer if they mind if you leave them unattended while you look after the new customer. Make sure you provide them with a helpful diversion, like product or service information, so that they do not feel their time is being wasted.

These are just a few ideas to illustrate this assessment criterion; you will need to find your own examples of how you deal with customers demanding your attention.

The final assessment criteria in learning outcome 1 relates to dealing with a customer who is adversely affecting the customer service enjoyed by other customers. We have all been in a shop or restaurant when a customer starts complaining or getting angry in an intrusive manner and this begins to affect the other customers around them. Whatever the cause of the disruption, it can create several scenarios:

- it becomes embarrassing for other customers

- other customers start to join in the argument or conversation

- the customer service professional becomes defensive and angry, setting a bad example and damaging the reputation of the organisation.

In a situation like this the customer service professional needs to:

- act assertively, not mirroring any aggression or anger
- separate the customer from others around them if possible, and take them to a quiet place
- calm the customer down and give them space
- ask them to explain the problem
- adopt an adult transactional state and deal with the facts of the situation
- listen and stay focused on what the customer is saying
- respond quietly but clearly
- ignore any rudeness on the customer's part
- empathise but do not patronise.

The evidence you need to produce for this unit could be an observation by your assessor of you working and interacting with your customers and colleagues. Observation with some questioning could capture most criteria in Learning Outcome 1. It is unlikely that your assessor will observe you for assessment criteria 1.7 and 1.8 but these could be evidenced through a personal statement/case study or professional discussion supported by a witness statement or an email of thanks. The information that you have prepared and collected from Performance evidence activities 1 and 2 and the examples you have prepared will help you to present some evidence for this learning outcome. You will need to discuss this with your assessor at the beginning of the qualification.

Performance evidence activity 2

Think of a scenario where you have had to calm down a situation when one customer was adversely affecting the customer service experience of others.

It might be a minor incident where a child was causing a nuisance to other customers or an internal customer reacted badly in a meeting. Make some notes so that you can develop this evidence with your assessor.

Figure A10.4: Focus on your customer

LO2 Improve the rapport with their customer through body language

Assessment criteria

2.1 Present a professional and respectful image when dealing with their customer

2.2 Show an awareness of their customer's needs for personal space

2.3 Focus their attention on their customer so that non-verbal signs do not betray disinterest, boredom or irritation

2.4 Ensure that their customer focus is not disrupted by colleagues

2.5 Observe all customers and the total customer service situation whilst maintaining rapport with their current customer

2.6 Observe their customer to read non-verbal clues about the customer's wishes and expectations

TUTORIAL 5 with your virtual advisor:

Much of the knowledge supporting assessment criteria 2.1 and 2.2 in this section has been discussed in Chapter 3 Unit A4 (assessment criterion 4.1 Describe their organisation's standards for appearance and behaviour). You looked at standards of dress, wearing of jewellery and the formality of the verbal language that is expected by the organisation and the customer. Earlier in this chapter, in Tutorial 1, we looked at creating rapport and a positive impression (assessment criterion 3.8). In Tutorial 2 we examined the principles of body language and how you and your customer are able to interpret this.

Assessment criteria 2.1 and 2.2 are best evidenced through observation, questioning and a quality check or witness statement from your manager or colleague. However, some of the answers that you have given to the questions and activities in this chapter could provide the basis for your performance evidence.

To meet the performance evidence requirements of assessment criteria 2.3 and 2.4 you will have to demonstrate that you focus on the customer and ignore distractions around you, such as ringing telephones or other conversations. Earlier on in Tutorial 1 you looked at active and empathetic listening skills and how you can use these to best effect when dealing with your customers. All of the points will help you to meet the assessment criteria and if you are observed by a manager or colleague and receive positive feedback this could go towards your evidence.

Finally, to meet the performance evidence requirements of assessment criteria 2.5 and 2.6 you will need to demonstrate the art of excellent customer service by using your powers of observation to take in everything that is going on around you while focusing on your current customer. You can do this by using your peripheral vision and all of your senses, but still maintaining eye contact and attention on what your customer is saying.

Distraction is easy at any time and if you are not connecting with your customer or you do not agree with what they are saying it is easy to lose concentration. Stay in touch with your body language and have an awareness of what you are doing; avoid fidgeting or fiddling or staring into space and try to block out the unimportant sounds around you. Keep focused on your customer's body language and look for clues that they might be confused or unhappy or their expectation might not be met.

Much of this behaviour can be observed by your assessor but they might want to follow it up with questions about how you recognised that the customer did not understand what you were saying or their wishes and expectations were not being met.

The next activity will help you to pull all of the preparation together and show your evidence through some 'live' examples of customer service transactions. Your explanation can be used in final evidence, but will need to be endorsed or supported by witnesses or work products.

Performance evidence activity 3

1. Reflect on a face-to-face transaction or meeting when there were a number of distractions from other customers or colleagues and you found it hard to give your full attention to the customer. How did you overcome the distractions and manage the situation?

2. Think about a transaction with a customer where you were aware that their body language indicated their wishes and expectations were not being met. What were the signs and how did you rescue the situation?

TUTORIAL 6 with your virtual advisor:

Evidence requirements provide the context in which you meet the assessment criteria for performance and enable your assessor to judge whether you are competent in a number of different situations. You do not need to cover the evidence requirements separately; they will be covered as you complete the assessment criteria. Your assessor will give you guidance. The **evidence requirements** for Unit A10 are explained below:

- *Your evidence must include examples of dealing with customers who:*
  - *have standard expectations of your organisation's customer service*
  - *have experienced difficulties when dealing with your organisation*
  - *have made a specific request for information*
  - *need to be informed of circumstances of which they are unaware.* To meet these evidence requirements you will need to provide examples of dealing with customers in all of the above contexts.

- *Your evidence must include examples of dealings with customers that are:*
  - *planned*
  - *unplanned.* This evidence requirement links with assessment criteria in learning outcome 1 where you are expected to plan a conversation with a customer and establish rapport. However, there will be times when your transaction is unplanned and you will still be expected to provide the same level of service to your customer. You will need to provide examples of both circumstances.

- *You must provide evidence of dealing with customers face to face during routine delivery of customer service.* This is when you are working in normal circumstances, not under extra pressure or dealing with unusual circumstances like holiday periods or seasonal surges (national holidays). You need to establish what is normal!

- *You must provide evidence of dealing with customers face to face during a busy time in your job.* Once you have decided on the routine delivery of customer service, you will be able to identify your busy times. Quite often you are aware of the times when you are busy and you can take this into consideration when selecting opportunities for your evidence collection. This will be a good opportunity to demonstrate assessment criteria 1.7 and 2.5.

- *You must provide evidence of dealing with customers face to face during a quiet time in your job.* In the same way you have identified busy times in your job, you can now identify when quiet times occur. Do you find things to do or do you sit around looking bored and does your body language convey this state of mind? Think about the impression you give to the customer. A proactive customer service professional will be able to provide a more individual service to customers when things are quiet and will have time to really focus on their needs and expectations. Think about the activities that you carry out when there is some downtime. Perhaps this is the time that you catch up on paperwork, cleaning and maintenance or carry out development activities. A busy person can look more professional; however, remember that when you do have a customer you will need to provide a positive impression of yourself and not display body language or facial expressions that indicate they are an intrusion on the activity being undertaken.

- *You must provide evidence of dealing with customers face to face when people, systems or resources have let you down.* There will be times when you cannot locate a colleague to ask about vital information and you will have to get back to your customer at a later date. A product might be out of stock even though computer records show that there are some available, or a colleague might have completed documentation incorrectly. These are the types of circumstances that you are likely to encounter that will meet this evidence requirement. Do you get anxious or impatient with the customer or are you giving out signals that you are stressed? Remember the body language you can communicate when affected by other people or inanimate objects like your computer. You will need to demonstrate calm and business-like behaviour, maintain rapport and avoid transferring your annoyance or irritation to the customer. The important thing to remember is how you create a positive impression under these circumstances.

A further part of the evidence requirements of this unit is the need to demonstrate that you communicate with customers using verbal and non-verbal communication skills.

- *You must include examples of how you have made use of:*
  - *verbal communication skills*
  - *non-verbal communication skills*. The customer transactions or meetings that you provide as evidence must demonstrate that you use both verbal skills (the most appropriate spoken language) and non-verbal skills (body language, facial expressions, positioning and posturing). This can be evidenced through observation, professional discussion or questioning.

The last activity is the learner evaluation. Each section in this chapter is intended to help you to develop yourself towards being a more thinking and reflective customer service professional. The learner evaluation requires you to reflect on your learning from completing this unit guide. Once again, this does not have to be written; however, it could be very useful to record your answers for use in reviews with your line manager, supervisor, assessor or tutor or possibly in a job interview.

Documenting your learning throughout your working life is a very effective way of showing that you use experience to influence your performance and behaviours. Reflect on what you knew at the start of the unit and what you know now.

1. What have you learned from completing this unit?

2. Identify three phrases that were new to you.

3. How will completing this unit affect your customer service within your organisation?

4. Highlight an improvement that you have made as a result of completing this unit.

If you are working towards Unit D3 Develop personal performance through delivering customer service, your evaluations might provide you with some foundation evidence.

Summary

This concludes the unit guidance for Unit A10 Deal with customers face to face.

You should be prepared to submit evidence for both the knowledge and performance aspects of the unit learning outcomes:

LO1: Communicate effectively with their customer
LO2: Improve the rapport with their customer through body language
LO3: Understand how to deal with customers face to face

You will now be able to describe how to deal with your customers face to face using positive body language, effective listening skills and how you create a rapport that will result in their wishes and expectations being met.

It is likely that the knowledge and performance evidence you produce for this unit will cross-reference to the following Customer Service units:

● Unit A4 Give your customer a positive impression of yourself and your organisation

● Unit B2 Deliver reliable customer service

● Unit C1 Recognise and deal with customer queries, requests and problems

● Unit D1 Develop customer relationships

● Unit F1 Communicate using customer service language

DEAL WITH INCOMING TELEPHONE CALLS FROM CUSTOMERS

Learning outcomes

Learning outcomes for Unit A11:
1. Use communication systems effectively
2. Establish rapport with customers who are calling
3. Deal effectively with customer questions and requests
4. Know how to deal with incoming telephone calls from customers

Introduction

This unit guide is a resource to help you gather the evidence that you require to achieve Unit A11, one of the optional units in the 'Impression and image' theme of the Level 2 NVQ Certificate in Customer Service. It can be used as a learning resource if you are new to your role, are studying customer service in preparation for work or as a refresher if you are an experienced customer service professional.

Deal with incoming telephone calls from customers – what is Unit A11 about?

Many organisations rely on dealing with incoming telephone calls as a key part of their customer service procedures. Customer expectations are high when calling organisations because they have had an opportunity to prepare for their call. In addition, a proportion of calls start with customers in a negative frame of mind because the caller sees making a call as a way of dealing with a customer service problem. This unit is about being prepared to deal effectively with calls and using effective communication to satisfy customers with the outcome of each call.

Source: Unit A11 purpose and aim

You will be able to demonstrate, through your work activities and your knowledge and understanding, how you receive incoming telephone calls effectively by using and maintaining the correct equipment. You will be able to show how you create a rapport through the use of appropriate language, effective listening skills and questioning and how you deal with your customers' requests to ensure their needs and expectations are met and their problems are resolved.

Completing this unit guide

To complete this unit guide you will need to:

1. Read through the information in each section.
2. Read the case study and reflective activity and use the questions to help you test your understanding.

There is no set format for working through or recording your answers in these sections, just use them in a way that suits your learning style, unless otherwise instructed by your assessor or tutor. The case study and reflective activity are linked to the assessment criteria in learning outcome 4, which focuses on the underpinning knowledge and understanding for Unit A11. Learning outcome 4 has been presented first so that you understand the background to the criteria in learning outcomes 1, 2 and 3. If you work through this section first you will find that your performance evidence will be easier to identify and present to your assessor.

Learning outcome 4 – Knowledge evidence

LO4 Know how to deal with incoming telephone calls from customers

- The tutorial section is designed to explain the assessment criteria. In this section your virtual advisor will provide you with information to help you interpret the national standards.

- The case study and reflective activity will help you to prepare to discuss and explain your understanding of customer service, with your assessor.

Learning outcomes 1, 2 and 3 – Performance evidence

- **LO1** Use communication systems effectively
- **LO2** Establish rapport with customers who are calling
- **LO3** Deal effectively with customer questions and requests.

In addition to the learning outcomes, in this unit there are performance **evidence requirements** that indicate the circumstances or conditions under which you should present the evidence.

You may provide evidence of dealing with customers using land line telephones, mobile telephones, internet telephone connections, video telephone systems or any other technology that involves a conversation with a customer at a distance.

Your evidence must include examples of dealing with customers who:

- have standard expectations of your organisation's customer service
- have experienced difficulties when dealing with your organisation
- have made a specific request for information
- need to be informed of circumstances of which they are unaware.

Your evidence must include examples of dealings with customers that are:

- planned
- unplanned.

You must provide evidence of dealing with customers by telephone:

- during routine delivery of customer service
- during a busy time in your job
- during a quiet time in your job
- when people, systems or resources have let you down.

You must provide evidence that you have taken messages that are passed on to colleagues:

- verbally
- in a form that maintains a permanent record.

Importance of providing effective telephone communication to customers

Customer service is not just a job; it underpins everything you do in your work role. If you are involved in providing products or services to others, whether internal or external to your organisation, via the telephone, it is essential that you are able to:

- operate and maintain the telephone equipment
- adapt your speech according to the needs of your customer
- demonstrate effective listening and questioning skills
- manage the telephone call in line with your organisation's guidelines.

The cycle of effective telephone communication

The cycle of effective telephone communication illustrates four important stages of the customer service transaction using voice communication at a distance. In Chapter 3 Unit A4 we looked at the communication cycle, although this was not specific to any one method. In this chapter we will look at your telephone interaction with your customers, both internal (i.e. colleagues, managers, service partners) and external to your organisation.

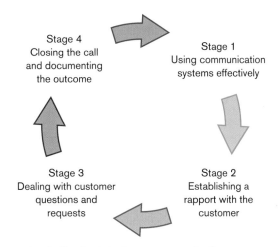

Figure A11.1: The cycle of effective telephone communication

Stage 1 Using communication systems effectively

Stage 1 is about having a thorough understanding of the telecommunications equipment that you operate in order to carry out your role of receiving incoming calls from a customer. The majority of communication will be via telephone – landlines and mobiles. However, the computer is increasingly becoming an alternative mode of linking with others, with new telecommunication technologies emerging, such as Voice over Internet Protocol, which involves speaking to others via the internet. Videoconferencing and visual (via webcam) instant messaging are already available to customers, both business and home users.

If you are using complex telecommunication hardware and software then your organisation should provide training and you should be able to access the relevant manuals and instruction material to familiarise yourself with the equipment and the procedures that are in place at work.

Stage 2 Establishing a rapport with the customer

It is vital that you concentrate on establishing a rapport between you and the customer. Rapport means finding and sharing common values, beliefs, knowledge or behaviours. In Chapter 3 Unit A4 we discussed expected standards of appearance and behaviour. When you communicate by telephone you need to conform to the telephone protocol of your organisation and your customer. You need to pay attention to the message you send out to your customer by your choice of words and phrases, the questions that you use, your pitch and tone of voice and your facial expression. All of these will have an impact on the overall impression you convey. Remember too that it is not just what you say that is important; think about the messages your customer provides to you and how you interpret them – make sure you use careful, active and empathetic listening.

Stage 3 Dealing with customer questions and requests

Stage 3 relates to making sure that the shape of the call is effective. This means that you listen to your customer's requests, questions or queries and use open, probing or closed questions to confirm your understanding and to process the information they give to you. It is about choosing the correct options and providing the information that the customer needs. It is also about taking command of the conversation so that it is timely and cost effective for both you and the customer.

Stage 4 Closing the call and documenting the outcome

The final stage of the cycle involves bringing the call to a close once you are satisfied the customer has sufficient information, their questions have been answered or they have been able to make a decision. Because you are not speaking face to face, it is vital to summarise your understanding of what has been discussed, both verbally and on your record system, and ensure that the customer is content with the outcome. It is important at this stage to complete any follow-up or fulfil any promises made to the customer.

Knowledge evidence for Unit A11 (LO4)

As stated earlier, we will begin with learning outcome 4 (LO4). This contains the knowledge criteria for the unit. In order to sustain and improve in your role as a customer service professional it is essential that you have this knowledge to underpin your performance.

LO4 Know how to deal with incoming telephone calls from customers

Assessment criteria

4.1 Describe their organisation's guidelines and procedures for the use of telecommunication equipment

4.2 Explain how to operate the organisation's telecommunication equipment

4.3 Explain the importance of speaking clearly and slowly when dealing with customers by telephone

4.4 Describe the effects of smiling and other facial expressions that can be detected by somebody listening to them on the telephone

4.5 Explain the importance of adapting their speech to meet the needs of customers who may find their language or accent difficult to understand

4.6 Identify what information is important to note during or after telephone conversations with customers

4.7 Describe their organisation's guidelines and procedures for what should be said during telephone conversations with customers

4.8 Explain the importance of keeping their customer informed if they are on hold during a call

4.9 Explain the importance of not talking across an open line

4.10 List details that should be included if taking a message for a colleague

4.11 Describe their organisation's guidelines and procedures for taking action to follow up calls made to customers

4.12 Describe their organisation's guidelines for handling abusive calls

TUTORIAL 1 with your virtual advisor:

Read through this tutorial so that you can meet the requirements of the assessment criteria shown above.

4.1 Describe their organisation's guidelines and procedures for the use of telecommunication equipment

4.2 Explain how to operate the organisation's telecommunication equipment

There are many types and brands of telecommunications systems in use in organisations and the equipment you use in your organisation will depend on the volume of calls you take, how long you are on the telephone and the products and services that you offer to your customers. The equipment will vary from a conventional telephone handset or mobile telephone to state-of-the-art videoconferencing equipment.

You must have a good understanding of the care and maintenance of telecommunications equipment so that you can deal with your customers promptly and effectively. This means regular cleaning of headsets, mouth pieces and key pads with the correct cleaning materials.

You need to understand how the equipment operates and the features and functions that you are expected to use, such as voicemail and call transfers. If you have not had any training on this then you might need to check with your supervisor that you are using the system in the correct way. Most systems will have a user manual in paper format or an online version – make sure you know where this is located.

There may be security features that you have to use when you sign in to the system and there may be health and safety requirements that you have to maintain, for example, only using *your* headset and cleaning it before and after use. If your main customer contact is via telephone you will also need to know what to do in case of an emergency situation when the telephone lines or equipment fail.

Questions

1. Explain the type of telephone system you use and its features and functions.

2. Identify the guidelines that you have been asked to follow for

   a) cleaning and maintaining the equipment

   b) logging in and starting up on the telephone line

   c) what you have to do if the telephone line or system fails.

3. List the security features on the telephone and why they are important.

4. Explain the step-by-step process of taking a routine call from a customer and how you operate the telephone equipment, for example, putting a customer on hold.

4.3 Explain the importance of speaking clearly and slowly when dealing with customers by telephone

4.5 Explain the importance of adapting their speech to meet the needs of customers who may find their language or accent difficult to understand

In the course of a day we speak to many people and often the interaction will be on the telephone. Depending on where you work, you will have to deal with a variety of customers, many of whom will have different communication needs. These needs could be linked to their age, language needs, culture and their prior knowledge of products or services. All of this has to be taken into consideration when you hold your conversation. As soon as you start the telephone conversation you make an assessment of the customer in the space of a few seconds. You have to make a decision on how to speak and what level and tone of voice to use, based only on the sound of the customer's voice, and you need to be clear and precise about what you want to say.

When dealing with a more mature customer do not assume that you have to talk loudly but also do not mumble. If you have a regional accent you need to be aware that not all customers will immediately be able to tune in to it and they may already be feeling apprehensive about the call and out of their comfort zone, particularly if they have gone through a push button process before they reach you. It is always advisable to speak slowly and clearly when you start the conversation; you can always adjust this once you have assessed the needs of your customer. Consider the timing and the speed of what you are saying; in the same way as talking too loudly or softly can impair the message, so can speaking too quickly or slowly.

Remember that some customers will be sensitive to background noises, particularly if they are calling from a mobile telephone or have their speakerphone on. Try to make sure that there is as little interference as possible from your end of the telephone line.

To sum up, it is important to speak clearly and slowly so that the message is conveyed to the customer with the least risk of misunderstanding or interference possible. When you evidence this assessment criterion you will need to bear the above in mind and explain the importance of speaking slowly and clearly, on the telephone, in the context of the customers that you deal with.

Questions

1. List three different types of customer that you speak to on the telephone.

2. What particular characteristics and needs do the customers have?

3. How do you adjust the way you talk to each of them according to their characteristics and needs?

4. Why is it important to adjust the language, pace and clarity of your speech with each of these customers?

4.4 Describe the effects of smiling and other facial expressions that can be detected by somebody listening to them on the telephone

When you talk to a customer face to face, smiling and facial expressions can affect their perception of you; this can also be picked up over the telephone because our facial muscles have an effect on the tone and pitch of our voice. Singers know that if they have a slight up-turn to the mouth or slight smile it can prevent them from going out of tune. This can be applied in a similar way on the telephone. By smiling you can develop a brighter and warmer resonance to your voice.

However, there is a difference between a slight smile and grinning, and your tone of voice should not sound flippant or imply that you are laughing at the customer. Other facial expressions may be detectable if they are accompanied by sighs or sharpness in tone as well. The effect that a smile will have on a customer can be very positive and they will respond by feeling that you care and are interested in what they are saying. It you are frowning or angry this will be picked up and the customer may feel that you have not got time for them.

Questions

1. Try a short experiment: ask a colleague to leave you two identical messages on your telephone – one where they are smiling and one where they are frowning. See if you can detect the smiling call and explain the effect that this had on you.

2. During two calls with your customers smile with one and have a straight face with the other. Did this affect the call in any way?

3. Write a short statement or prepare some notes from the experiments about the effects that smiling or other facial expressions have on your customers. Explain the outcome to your assessor.

4.6 Identify what information is important to note during or after telephone conversations with customers

You will be expected to prepare your place of work or work station before you start dealing with your customers. It is often difficult to recall details of a call afterwards, so it is always advisable to make notes as you go along. Therefore, it is important that you have a pen and note pad or a facility on your computer to take down information during and after a telephone call. You might have set processes or procedures for documenting this information.

Questions

1. Select two telephone calls and identify the information that you found useful to note during or after the telephone conversations with your customers.

2. Explain your reasons for making the records.

Figure A11.2: Following organisation guidelines for incoming calls

4.7 Describe their organisation's guidelines and procedures for what should be said during telephone conversations with customers

As customers we find ourselves making calls to various organisations, often on a daily basis, for example:

- to make an appointment at the doctor, dentist or hairdresser
- to ask for information and advice from banks, mobile telephone providers and insurance companies
- to purchase or complain about products and services.

Opening the call: Often a customer telephoning an organisation will have to go through a series of automated stages and enter information before they speak to a real person. While this is a cost effective filter for an organisation it has an impact on customer satisfaction and each time they call they want to be reassured that they are through to the right company and a person who can help them. Some organisations are better than others at giving the customer this information. They will provide a greeting, their company name, their own name and ask the customer how they can help. It is important that you are aware of the guidelines that your organisation provides for the opening of a telephone call and how you should apply them.

During the call: There will be other guidelines that you have to follow depending on the products and services offered to your customers. Many of these guidelines will be linked to legal information that must be conveyed to the customer, while others will be linked into the service offers and promises that you make to your customers. For example, a customer service professional working in an insurance call centre will need to advise customers about the need to answer questions truthfully and that they have a period of time (normally 14 days) to change their mind about the policy. In a bank call centre the customer will be asked information about their address and date of birth to comply with data protection and they usually have to provide secure details about themselves to prove their identity.

Call wrap up/closing the call: This will often require the customer service professional to provide summary information and the way forward, or actions to be taken. There might be some set phrases or information that you have to provide at this stage of the call but more importantly, you should let the customer know that you have valued their time and custom and that you are interested in what they have asked or told you. Leave the customer feeling satisfied that you have focused on their needs and are there to help them.

Question

1. Describe the guidelines and procedures set by your organisation for what should be said:
   a) at the call opening
   b) during the call
   c) at close of call

4.8 Explain the importance of keeping their customer informed if they are on hold during a call

4.9 Explain the importance of not talking across an open line

What is an open telephone line? It is when you are on a telephone call and the customer is not on hold or you have not muted your line to avoid the customer hearing what you are saying.

During a call you might have to speak to a colleague for advice or guidance, transfer the customer to another department, look up some information situated away from the telephone or collect your thoughts while you make a decision. It is important to put your customer on hold so that they are not listening to the conversation in the background or left waiting too long.

Many offices and shops are busy and noisy; there may be a number of people talking in the background or taking telephone calls at the same time as you, and although the telephone microphone does not pick up everything there can be times when someone in the background shouts or talks loudly and your customer might overhear what is being said.

Alternatively, you might need to ask a colleague about a problem. If you have to do this it is not advisable to leave the telephone line open or to put your hand over the mouthpiece to muffle the sound. Use the hold or mute button to cut out the customer. This is particularly important if you have to explain confidential or restricted information or if you are going to speak to a colleague about the customer's behaviour. If your customer overhears you then it might cause unnecessary stress or upset. When you put a customer on hold it is vital that you provide an indication of how long you will be and also what you are going to do for them. If the hold time is likely to exceed the time indicated by you, then you should go back and explain what is happening. Your customer is less likely to get impatient if you keep them informed.

Questions

1. Explain the process for putting customers on hold during a telephone call.

2. Describe two instances of when you put a customer on hold and why it was necessary to do this.

3. What could have happened if you had not put them on hold and left the telephone line open?

Figure A11.3

4.10 List details that should be included if taking a message for a colleague

When taking any type of message for a colleague, it should be clear and succinct and there should be a beginning, middle and end. The beginning should highlight when the message was taken, the time and date and by whom. The body of the message should have a brief description of what was required by the caller and the end should summarise any actions or targets promised or requested.

Question

1. Provide two examples of messages that you have taken for colleagues. What did you have to include in the message?

2. How did you document and communicate it to them?

4.11 Describe their organisation's guidelines and procedures for taking action to follow up calls made to customers

There will be occasions when you miss a call from a customer and they request you call them back or you are unable to resolve a query, request or problem for a customer in one telephone conversation. When the latter happens you might have agreed certain actions to be undertaken by yourself or your colleagues before you call the customer back. There are several issues to take into consideration when this happens:

- What timeframe did you give to the customer?
- Was it realistic and achievable?
- How will you remind yourself to get back to them?
- When will you get back to them?

You must keep the promises you make to the customer and assume responsibility for getting back to the customer within the promised time frame. If this is not possible, then an update or progress call should be made so that you do not disappoint the customer. They may be waiting by the telephone for you to call back, so you need to bear this in mind. A customer would much rather be informed about what is happening even if the situation is not completely resolved.

Question

- Describe the guidelines and procedures in place for follow up calls to your customers.

4.12 Describe their organisation's guidelines for handling abusive calls

There are two types of abusive calls: 1) abusive or nuisance calls where the sole purpose of the caller is to be rude or malicious; 2) when the customer gets angry or frustrated and the abusive behaviour develops during the course of the conversation. This can be more distressing than the former as one minute the customer is speaking normally and then suddenly they start to swear or become aggressive.

It is important that you know and understand the limits of tolerance and when to close the call. Any form of abusive call can be distressing, but it is important not to take the call content personally.

- Listen and do not interrupt or talk over the caller.
- Remain cool and calm and try to talk the customer round.
- If they are not responding positively, personalise the conversation by calling them by name, if you know it, repeat your name and that you want to do everything you can to help them.
- Remind the customer you can only help them if they do not use bad language and talk reasonably to you.
- If they become more abusive or you can see that the conversation is going round in circles it might be advisable to transfer them to a supervisor and explain to them where and why you are transferring them.
- If there is no one to transfer them to and they are extremely abusive and unlikely to calm down, explain that you want to help them but your organisation does not allow customer service professionals to continue in an abusive conversation and ask them to call back another time before closing the call.

Questions

1. Identify your organisation's guidelines for dealing with aggressive or abusive telephone calls.

2. If you have experienced an abusive call explain how you dealt with it.

3. Based on this experience how would you handle a similar call in the future?

Now read the case study below and answer the questions that follow to consolidate some of the information covered in Tutorial 1. You do not have to write your answers down unless your tutor or assessor has asked you to do so.

CASE STUDY 1 Call for Candice

Candice is an ex-nurse and works in a call centre for a health helpline service. On a regular shift she will handle a number of calls from her customers – members of the public who have health concerns but are reluctant to call an ambulance and cannot get to their local GP. Candice's knowledge of nursing comes in very useful and there are stringent guidelines of what she can and cannot advise a customer to do and when she has to contact her service partners or colleagues for help. The call centre has staff working 24 hours a day, seven days a week.

The desks are shared, so when Candice arrives for work she has to adjust her chair and the height of her desk and clean down her workstation with sterilising wipes. She collects her headphones and logs into her computer using a password because the information that she keeps is highly confidential. She has ten minutes to set her workstation up and this includes opening her three visual display units, (her computer screens and a digital telephone display known as an automatic call distributor). She also opens up a number of software packages, health-related references, maps and directories on the internet/intranet. As soon as she is fully prepared she has to go into a state of 'ready', meaning she is able to take calls.

The calls that come through are varied in terms of urgency and the types of customers. Some of the customers are very distressed and anxious and Candice ensures that she deals with all of them according to their needs. Candice was born and lived in Newcastle until she was twenty years old; she is aware that she has a strong regional accent. Some of her customers do not speak English as a first language so she is careful to use phrases and expressions that they will understand; she always checks that they are happy with the speed and clarity of her speech.

Candice processes the calls and uses the information she has onscreen to advise her customers and she makes referrals to GP practices and the ambulance service if there is a need for the customer to be seen by a medical expert. During the call she has a database of questions that she asks each customer in order to build a full picture of their needs and health history. Candice makes notes on her screen and sets up a customer record for each caller. From time to time she has to get information from her team leader. She always makes sure that she puts her customer's call on hold as she does not want her customer to hear the other confidential conversations that are going on in the call centre; she lets her customer know what she is doing. At the end of the call she provides the customer with a call reference number and explains what action needs to be taken by them or will be taken by her service partners (ambulance paramedics, doctors or other medical experts).

After each call Candice goes into a state of 'after call' which means she is still logged into the call but has a chance to complete the documentation and organise any follow up action. She tries to make sure she completes this effectively and within the guidelines for the length of call. Occasionally she will have to contact the customer to explain the next steps in the process. This is usually because she has not been able to contact a doctor to ask for advice or to request a home visit to the customer. She always tells the customer when she will get back to them and sets an alert in her diary system to remind herself.

Occasionally a customer will be so distressed they will become abusive. Candice follows her organisation's guidelines in these instances and tries to calm the customer. If their language becomes unacceptable she tells them she is here to help them and they have the option of behaving reasonably or she will have to terminate the call. If they do not respond she will tell them that they can call their doctor when the surgery is open and she provides them with the times and telephone numbers, or if the situation is urgent then they need to call the emergency services. She explains that there is a zero tolerance policy for abusive behaviour within the ambulance service. She will then close the call if there is no improvement in their attitude.

Questions

1. How does Candice prepare for her shift and what health and safety checks and actions does she take?

2. What precautions does Candice take to maintain security of information?

3. How does Candice check her customers understand what she is saying?

4. Where does Candice record her call information?

5. How does Candice maintain good customer service with abusive callers?

The reflective activity below is designed to start you thinking about your reactions and feelings when you have encountered different customer service scenarios. The activity is from the perspective of you as the customer. We are all customers on a regular basis and this activity will help to prepare you to collect evidence that will demonstrate your knowledge, understanding and practical skills in customer service. You can write down your reflections if you wish as you may find them useful in discussions or questioning sessions with your assessor or in the preparation of your evidence.

REFLECTIVE ACTIVITY

1. Analyse a recent telephone conversation when you were the customer and the customer service professional created a good rapport.

2. Now think of a time when you experienced a telephone transaction where you felt uncomfortable about the way the customer service professional dealt with your needs and expectations.

3. In the case of the positive experience, what did the customer service professional do to create rapport?

4. In the case of the negative experience, what did the customer service professional do that caused you to feel uncomfortable?

If you cannot think of your own scenarios, speak to a friend, colleague or your tutor and ask them about their experiences.

Performance evidence for Unit A11 (LO1, LO2, LO3)

The case study and reflective activity have given you the opportunity to consider the customer service provided by a customer service professional and to think about customer expectations from your own experiences.

The next section in this unit is designed to help you focus on the learning outcomes and performance requirement of Unit A11 and prompt you to think how you can evidence it through your customer service role. It is expected that the evidence that you generate for this unit will also cross-reference with some of the optional units that you have selected. The virtual advisor will guide you to collect the evidence that you need to complete this unit.

LO1 Use communication systems effectively

Assessment criteria

1.1 Operate telecommunication equipment efficiently and effectively
1.2 Speak clearly and slowly and adapt their speech to meet the individual needs of their customer
1.3 Listen carefully when collecting information from their customer
1.4 Select the information they need to record and store following their organisation's guidelines
1.5 Update their customer records during or after the call to reflect the key points of the conversation

Much of the knowledge supporting the assessment criteria for learning outcome 1 has been discussed earlier in this chapter in learning outcome 4, where we looked at establishing rapport and listening to your customer. We recapped on the importance of awareness of your organisation's policies and procedures and how they impact on telephone transactions. You might have already answered some of the questions in previous tutorials in this chapter. If you have gathered some examples from your own work situation these could be expanded to contribute to your performance evidence.

The first assessment criterion in LO1 is about the preparations that you make before you start to deal with your customers. The remaining criteria are best observed by your assessor. Some of the notes that you have prepared from your activities in LO4 will help to form a basis for you to answer questions or to have a professional discussion with your assessor.

LO2 Establish rapport with customers who are calling

Assessment criteria

2.1 Greet their customer following their organisation's guidelines
2.2 Listen closely to their customer to identify their precise reason for calling and what outcome they are seeking from the call
2.3 Confirm the identity of their customer following organisational guidelines
2.4 Use effective and assertive questions to clarify their customer's requests

The assessment criteria in learning outcome 2 consider the telephone transaction in more detail, from the opening stages of the greeting to establishing the purpose of the call, the needs of the customer and obtaining their details if they are necessary to the transaction.

Assertive and professional behaviour is examined in Chapter 4 Unit A10 (Tutorial 2) and in Chapter 8 Unit D1 (Tutorial 2). In this instance you must demonstrate that you ask your customer effective questions and that you take control of the telephone call in a firm and positive way, without being aggressive.

How do you ensure that you ask effective questions? It is important that you have an understanding of some of the basic techniques of questioning. There are several types of questions that you can ask a customer depending on what information you need from them.

Open questions are useful at the start of the conversation to gather information. If you use What? Why? Where? How? or When? to start your question this will enable the customer to respond with the information that you need. For example, 'How can I help you?'

Probing questions help you to develop the conversation further. If you use words like 'tell', 'explain' and 'describe', this enables the customer to provide supplementary information about their feelings and expectations. For example: 'Please describe the fault on the computer.'

Closed questions are phrased so that you get a 'yes' or 'no' answer. They are particularly useful if you are trying to check your customer's understanding of the information or solution that you have given them. For example: 'Are you satisfied with the new delivery date?'

Once again observation will be the best evidence for the criteria in learning outcome 2, but you can support this through the notes or personal statements you have produced for the LO4 knowledge activities earlier in this chapter.

Performance evidence activity 1

1. Provide two examples of open questions that you have used with your customers.

2. Provide two examples of probing questions that you have used with your customers.

3. How and why do you use closed questions in your telephone calls with customers? Provide two examples of closed questions.

LO3 Deal effectively with customer questions and requests

Assessment criteria

3.1 Identify all the options they have for responding to their customer and weigh up the benefits and drawbacks of each

3.2 Choose the option that is most likely to lead to customer satisfaction within the service offer

3.3 Give clear and concise information to customers in response to questions or requests

3.4 Use questions and answers to control the length of the conversation

3.5 Keep their customer regularly informed about their actions when accessing information to provide responses or if they are going to be on hold for a period of time

3.6 Put their customer on hold and ensure they cannot be heard if they are discussing action with others or calling a colleague

3.7 Summarise the outcome of the call and any actions that they or their customer will take as a result

3.8 Check before the call is finished that their customer is content that all their questions or requests have been dealt with

3.9 Complete any follow up actions agreed during the call

3.10 Take a clear message for a colleague if they are unable to deal with some aspect of their customer's questions or requests

3.11 Ensure that promises to call back are kept

TUTORIAL 4 with your virtual advisor:

Much of the knowledge supporting the assessment criteria for learning outcome 3 has been discussed in learning outcome 4 earlier in the chapter. The criteria in LO3 break down the process of the telephone conversation into stages. However, when you deal with your customer you will be making rapid decisions at each stage. The only way that you can carry this out effectively is by knowing your products and services, your processes and procedures, the limits of the service offer and when you can be flexible to meet customer requirements.

You will need to provide evidence of a number of calls that you have dealt with over time with your customers. This can be evidenced through observation by your assessor or through activities such as quality checks, one-to-one meetings or recordings of the calls that you have made. If the recordings are not accessible to your assessor, your manager or supervisor may be able to provide a statement (verbal or written) to support your work performance against the assessment criteria. Discuss the best option with your assessor.

TUTORIAL 5 with your virtual advisor:

Evidence requirements provide the context in which you meet the assessment criteria for performance and enable your assessor to judge whether you are competent in a number of different situations. You do not need to cover the evidence requirements separately; they will be covered as you complete the assessment criteria. Your assessor will give you guidance. The evidence requirements for Unit A11 are explained below.

● *You may provide evidence of dealing with customers using land line telephones, mobile telephone, internet telephone connections, video telephone systems or any other technology that involves a conversation with a customer at a distance. The type of telephony equipment that you use should be covered in this evidence requirement. If it is not, talk to your assessor to check that this unit matches your job role.*

● *Your evidence must include examples of dealing with customers who:*
   – *have standard expectations of your organisation's customer service*
   – *have experienced difficulties when dealing with your organisation*
   – *have made a specific request for information*
   – *need to be informed of circumstances of which they are unaware.* All of these evidence requirements will be applied in the context of dealing with your customers over the telephone. You could, for instance, provide an example of a straightforward call from a customer; a call where the customer has been locked into a queue but needed to get through to you and did not want to abandon the call; an example when the customer was requesting

some information and knew what they wanted; and a call when you were aware (perhaps from the customer's records on your database) of a problem or missing information that your customer did not have access to and that would impact on the quality of the customer service they received.

- *Your evidence must include examples of dealings with customers that are:*
  - *planned*
  - *unplanned.*

    This evidence requirement links with assessment criteria in learning outcomes 1 and 2 where you are expected to open and conduct your call using your organisation's guidelines. However, there will be times when your transaction is unplanned and you will still be expected to provide the same level of service to your customer. You will need to provide examples of both circumstances.

- *You must provide evidence of dealing with customers by telephone during routine delivery of customer service.* This is when you are working in normal circumstances, not under extra pressure or dealing with unusual circumstances like holiday periods or seasonal surges (national holidays). You need to establish what is normal!

- *You must provide evidence of dealing with customers by telephone during a busy time in your job.* Once you have decided on the routine delivery of customer service, you will be able to identify your busy times. You should be able to refer to your call statistics to identify when you are busy and you can take this into consideration when selecting opportunities for your evidence collection. This will be a good opportunity to demonstrate assessment criteria 1.1–1.5.

- *You must provide evidence of dealing with customers by telephone during a quiet time in your job.* In the same way you have identified busy times in your job, you can now identify when quiet times occur. Do you find things to do or do you sit around looking bored and does your tone of voice convey this state of mind? Think about the impression you give to the customer. A proactive customer service professional will be able to provide a more individual service to customers when things are quiet and will have time to focus on their needs and expectations. Think about the activities that you carry out when there is some downtime. Perhaps this is the time that you catch up on updating notes about your customers or cleaning and maintaining your telecommunications equipment. However, remember that when you do have a customer you will need to use appropriate communication techniques and not indicate they are an intrusion on the activity you are undertaking.

- *You must provide evidence of dealing with customers by telephone when people, systems or resources have let you down.* There will be times when you cannot locate a colleague to ask about vital information and you will have to get back to your customer at a later date or your telecommunications system may develop a problem or break down. These are the types of circumstances that you are likely to encounter that will meet this evidence requirement. You will need to demonstrate calm and business-like behaviour, maintain rapport and avoid indicating your annoyance or irritation to the customer by the tone of your voice or the phrases that you use. The important thing to remember is how you create a positive impression under these circumstances.

A further part of the evidence requirements of this unit is the need to demonstrate that you have taken messages that are passed on to colleagues.

- *You must provide evidence that you have taken messages that are passed on to colleagues:*
  - *verbally*
  - *in a form that maintains a permanent record.* The messages that you provide as evidence must demonstrate that you use verbal skills (the most appropriate spoken language) and show that the form you have chosen will provide a permanent record. This can be evidenced through observation or discussion, looking at products of message taking.

Your examples of evidence, through observation, personal statement supported by documents and customer records or witness statements, must cover all of the contexts and circumstances listed in the evidence requirements.

Performance evidence activity 2 will help you to pull all of the preparation together and show your evidence through some 'live' examples of customer service transactions. Your explanation can be used in final evidence but will need to be endorsed or supported by witnesses or work products.

Performance evidence activity 2

To meet the requirements of this unit you will need to make some written notes about how you have dealt with the following situations.

1. A planned telephone transaction with a customer who has standard expectations of your organisation's customer service during routine delivery of customer service.

2. An unplanned telephone transaction with a customer who has experienced difficulties when dealing with your organisation. This could have been caused by people, systems or resources that have let you and/or the customer down.

3. A planned or unplanned transaction when the customer has made a specific request for information. This could be during routine delivery of customer service or during a busy or quiet time in your job.

4. A planned or unplanned transaction when the customer needs to be informed of circumstances of which they are unaware.

5. An example of taking a call and passing a message to a colleague a) verbally b) in a permanent format.

If you have difficulty in finding examples that match the requested performance evidence activity then talk to your assessor about how you can meet the outstanding evidence requirements. You might have examples from past work performance or there could be evidence from observations carried out for other units, particularly A4, B2, D1 and C1.

Summary

This concludes the unit guidance for A11 Deal with incoming telephone calls from customers.

You should be prepared to submit evidence for both the knowledge and performance aspects of the unit learning outcomes:

LO1: Use communication systems effectively
LO2: Establish rapport with customers who are calling
LO3: Deal effectively with customer questions and requests
LO4: Know how to deal with incoming telephone calls from customers

You will now be able to describe how you prepare to deal with customers by telephone. You will be able to explain and demonstrate how you make contact and act assertively and professionally, creating a rapport with the customer. Finally you will be able to show how effectively you deal with the questions and requests that your customers present to you.

It is likely that the knowledge and performance evidence you produce for this unit will cross-reference to the following Customer Service units:

- Unit A4 Give your customer a positive impression of yourself and your organisation

- Unit B2 Deliver reliable customer service

- Unit C1 Recognise and deal with customer queries, requests and problems

- Unit D1 Develop customer relationships.

Learning outcomes

Learning outcomes for Unit B2:

1. Prepare to deal with customers
2. Give consistent service to customers
3. Check customer service delivery
4. Know how to deliver reliable customer service

Introduction

This unit guide is a resource to help you gather the evidence that you require to achieve Unit B2, one of the optional units in the Delivery theme of the Level 2 NVQ Certificate in Customer Service. It can be used as a learning resource if you are new to your role, are studying customer service in preparation for work or as a refresher if you are an experienced customer service professional.

Deliver reliable customer service – what is Unit B2 about?

It is about how you deliver consistent and reliable service to customers. As well as being good with people, you need to work with your organisation's service systems to meet or exceed customer expectations. In your job there will be many examples of how you combine your approach and behaviour with your organisation's systems. You will need to prepare for each transaction with a customer, deal with different types of customers in different circumstances and check that what you have done has met customer expectations. To meet this standard you have to deliver excellent customer service over and over again.

Source: Adapted from Unit B2 purpose and aim

You will be able to demonstrate through your work activities how you ensure that your work area is tidy, safe and organised ready for you to deal with your customers. You will be able to show how you prepare and carry out your customer service transactions. You will be able to evidence the feedback from customers that indicates their level of satisfaction about the service they receive and share this with your managers, colleagues and others in your organisation in order to make improvements.

Completing this unit guide

To complete this unit guide you will need to:

1. Read through the information in each section.
2. Look at the case study and reflective activity and use the questions to help you to test your understanding.

There is no set format for working through or recording your answers in these sections, just use them in a way that suits your learning style, unless otherwise instructed by your assessor or tutor. The case study and reflective activity are linked to the assessment criteria in learning outcome 4, which focuses on the underpinning knowledge and understanding for Unit B2. Learning outcome 4 has been presented first so that you understand the background to the assessment criteria in learning outcomes 1, 2 and 3. If you work through this section first you will find that your performance evidence will be easier to identify and present to your assessor.

Learning outcome 4 – Knowledge evidence

LO4 Know how to deliver reliable customer service

- The tutorial section is designed to explain the assessment criteria. In this section your virtual advisor will provide you with information to help you interpret the national standards.
- The case study and reflective activity will help you to prepare to discuss and explain your understanding of customer service with your assessor.

Learning outcomes 1, 2 and 3 – Performance evidence

- **LO1** Prepare to deal with customers
- **LO2** Give consistent service to customers
- **LO3** Check customer service delivery

In addition to the learning outcomes, in this unit there are performance **evidence requirements** that indicate the circumstances or conditions under which you should present the evidence.

You must provide evidence that you have worked with different customers who have different needs and expectations.

You must provide evidence of delivering reliable customer service:

- during routine delivery of customer service
- during a busy time in your job
- during a quiet time in your job
- when people, systems or resources have let you down.

Why do I need to deliver reliable customer service?

Customer service is not just a job; it underpins everything you do in your work role. If you are involved in providing products or services to others, internal or external to your organisation, it is essential that you are able to:

- keep your knowledge of products and services up to date
- ensure that the environment in which you work is safe, tidy and ready for your customers
- provide a consistent service to your customers according to their needs and expectations
- evaluate the service that you have provided through feedback
- identify areas for improvement and share this information with colleagues and service partners.

The cycle of reliable customer service delivery

The cycle of reliable customer service delivery illustrates four important stages of any customer service transaction regardless of the setting.

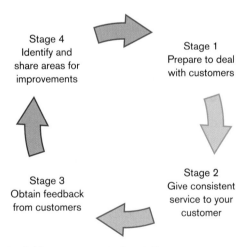

Figure B2.1: The cycle of reliable customer service delivery

Stage 1 Prepare to deal with customers

You must be fully prepared to deal with your customers – in other words, you must be ready, willing and able to deliver according to demand. To support this you will need a comprehensive and up-to-date knowledge of your products and services. In Chapter 1 Unit F1 we looked at the need to be inquisitive or curious about the products and services, rules, procedures and the legal guidelines that impact on your customer service provision. This includes areas such as health and safety and security of property and information.

Stage 2 Give consistent service to your customers

You will be expected to know and understand the limits of the service you can deliver so that you make realistic promises to your customer. This stage is also about being honest with your customer and communicating to them if and when circumstances change, or you are unable to deliver on time.

Stage 3 Obtain feedback from customers

Stage 3 is the most important stage of the cycle. Without feedback it is impossible to tell (before it is too late) whether you have met customer expectations and needs. The feedback can be in a number of ways, such as simple questioning, surveys and questionnaires, compliments and complaints.

Stage 4 Identify and share areas for improvements

Stage 4 is about doing something positive with the feedback you receive, for example, sharing it with colleagues and service partners so that you learn from your customers what delights them (value for money, speed of delivery or convenience, for example) and when they are less than satisfied. The best ideas for improvement can often come from your customers as they are the end user. Obtaining feedback is an opportunity for you and your organisation to demonstrate that you listen to customers, question them and take action. The cycle of reliable customer service is a continuous process: you should always be preparing, delivering, requesting feedback and making changes and improvements.

Knowledge evidence for Unit B2 (LO4)

As stated earlier, we will begin with learning outcome 4 (LO4). This contains the knowledge criteria for the unit. In order to sustain and improve in your role as a customer service professional it is essential that you have this knowledge to underpin your performance.

LO4 Know how to deliver reliable customer service

Assessment criteria

4.1 Describe their organisation's services or products
4.2 Explain their organisation's procedures and systems for delivering customer service
4.3 Describe methods or systems for measuring an organisation's effectiveness in delivering customer service
4.4 Explain their organisation's procedures and systems for checking service delivery
4.5 Explain their organisation's requirements for health and safety in their area of work

Read through this tutorial so that you can meet the requirements of the assessment criteria shown above.

4.1 Describe their organisation's services or products

The need to familiarise yourself with the products and services that you deliver is covered in Chapter 1 Unit F1, Chapter 4 Unit A10 and in Chapter 8 Unit D1. For assessment criteria 4.1 you have to be able to describe your organisation's products and services; this may include products and services outside of your remit but of interest to customers. This information may be readily available to you through training, day-to-day tasks like unpacking stock or emails from suppliers, colleagues and service partners. However, you must be curious and seek information in addition to the sources described above in order to be totally prepared for any questions, information or requests that your customer might make. For example, this might be a new version of a product being released in the near future, updated software or changes in procedures that might affect the service you provide.

The internet is ideal for researching new developments, product updates, training materials, factual information or to see what your competitors are doing. Use trade or professional magazines and journals and talk to experts, developers, managers and trainers so that you get a wider perspective of the sector or market that you are operating within.

Consider the following questions in relation to your customer service situation. Making notes will help you to collect your thoughts and you can use them when you meet with your 'live' assessor or tutor.

Questions

1. Describe three products or services unique to your area of work and identify where you already have, or can obtain, information to extend your knowledge about the products.

2. Talk to a manager or expert in your organisation (or look at the internet or any other sources available) to see if there are any developments, new models or advice that might have an impact on the information your customers will request about the three products or services you identified.

To satisfy this assessment criterion you will need to be able to describe all of your organisation's products and services to your assessor. However, it is possible that they might observe you describing some of them to your customers as well.

Figure B2.2: Be curious, seek new information for your customers

4.2 Explain their organisation's procedures and systems for delivering customer service

In Chapter 1 Unit F1 you looked at the importance of knowing and understanding the products and services that you deliver and how effective procedures are essential to ensure that service is delivered to consistent standards. It is vital that you have a sound understanding of the procedures that you and your colleagues and service partners use and you understand why they are there. These procedures could relate to complaints, after care and servicing and delivery of goods and services. There will be some procedures that are directly relevant to your area of responsibility and others that you should have an awareness of.

Questions

1. Make a list of all of the procedures that you have to use and describe how they work.

2. Identify at least two procedures that you are aware of in your organisation, not used directly by you. How do they impact on you and your department, section or branch?

4.3 Describe methods or systems for measuring an organisation's effectiveness in delivering customer service

Stage 3 of the cycle of reliable customer service delivery focuses on obtaining feedback from customers to establish levels of satisfaction with products and services. A proactive organisation will ensure that they have good processes in place to gather data and information about customer satisfaction.

It is important that you are familiar with the feedback systems in your organisation so that you can use them when appropriate. Often there are formal processes for collecting feedback, for example, a customer satisfaction questionnaire, a comments box or a set of questions that are asked at the end of every transaction. Many online retailers use a review system and send an email to the customer requesting feedback after they have purchased a product. The feedback is posted online so that other customers can use it to help them make a decision. However, both positive and negative feedback is published and the organisation cannot do anything to prevent negative feedback appearing. It is therefore good practice to have a system in place that will allow a customer service professional to respond to negative comments as soon as possible and take action to resolve the issues or problems that the customer has complained about.

Many organisations have quality assurance checks in place. Often these are carried out by managers and supervisors, but in some cases they will be conducted by mystery shoppers (people who pose as a regular customer but will be assessing you or your organisation). In all cases the customer service will be assessed against key points essential to service delivery. The criteria might be linked to the service offer, customer promise, standards of service or service level agreements; we discussed these in Chapter 1, Tutorial 2.

Question

1. When you next use a bank, mobile phone operator, restaurant, retailer or shop online, look for their service delivery checks. Identify two different customer service measures that you have come across.

Figure B2.3

4.4 Explain their organisation's procedures and systems for checking service delivery

In every customer service transaction there are clues contained in verbal and written comments, body language and facial expressions that indicate customer satisfaction. It is up to the customer service professional to develop a 'sixth sense' and use this information to check if the service has met their requirements. Follow up comments with questions and write down some of the casual remarks (positive and negative) you receive; you might find there are common themes of thanks and satisfaction or areas that need improvement.

If your organisation has a mystery shopper check or any other form of quality assurance checks in place you should be getting either individual or team feedback from this source.

Question

1. Identify all of the feedback systems that exist in your organisation and explain how they are used to check service delivery. If you cannot find anything in place in your organisation ask your manager and offer to set up a system of recording and monitoring verbal or written comments made about your products and services.

4.5 Explain their organisation's requirements for health and safety in their area of work

Health and safety underpins everything that we undertake in the work place. We discussed this in more depth in Chapter 2 Unit F2. Under the terms of the Health and Safety at Work Act 1974 you have a right to work in an area where risks to your health and safety are properly controlled. However, it is not just the responsibility of your manager or employer to control this risk.

You have a responsibility to:

- follow the health and safety training that you have been given at work
- take reasonable care of your own and other people's health and safety
- report anything that you think could put your customers, colleagues, visitors or your own health and safety at risk.

You have a responsibility to take care of your area of work and monitor it for health and safety at all times – often known as housekeeping.

Your organisation should have trained you and informed you at the start of your employment what was required of you in terms of keeping your desk or work area tidy, disposing of waste, dealing with spills, storing resources and products, fire and other emergency procedures. If you are not familiar with or cannot remember these requirements then you might need to refresh your knowledge.

If you deal with customers face to face you will need to be aware of how your behaviour could impact on their wellbeing. If you provide information to customers, whether over the phone or in writing, you will need an awareness of the impact of providing incorrect information to them. This is known as risk assessment and should be discussed on a regular basis with your manager and colleagues.

Question

1. Prepare some notes so that you can explain your organisation's health and safety requirements for:

   ● fire and emergency situations

   ● waste disposal

   ● cleaning and maintenance of the work area

   ● storage

   ● smoking

   ● reporting of accidents

   ● hazard reporting.

The case study below provides an opportunity for you to read about a customer service professional and consolidates some of the information from the tutorial. You can use this to reflect on the situation and answer some questions. You do not have to write your answers down unless your tutor or assessor has asked you to do so.

CASE STUDY 1: The PCSO

Simon is a police community support officer (PCSO) for Westchester Constabulary. There is a strong customer service dimension to his job and this is reflected in the policing plan published by the Chief Constable of Westchester Constabulary to members of the community. The plan outlines how Simon and his fellow officers will provide an excellent service by:

● improving community engagement

● visiting victims of crime

● providing reassurance to the community.

Simon has responsibility for the rural area of Sandford. His external customers are the local community members and residents, community organisations such as youth clubs, neighbourhood watch and the local schools. His internal customers are colleagues and fellow officers in Westchester Constabulary.

The purpose of Simon's role as a PCSO is to improve the community and offer greater public reassurance and this is published on the organisation's website. He works alongside his colleagues who are regular police officers. Simon patrols the area of Sandford and provides a visible and accessible uniformed presence to the community members. He works with community organisations to reduce anti-social behaviour and fear of crime and deals with environmental and other issues which affect people living in the community. For example, Simon will investigate reports of vandalism and suspicious activity. He provides crime prevention advice at meetings known as beat surgeries and visits people who have been victims of crime, to provide support and reassurance.

Simon has access to the policing records system, but under data protection laws can only access details of crimes that he has been involved in reporting or documenting. He is not allowed to name anyone involved in a crime but does have access to statistics on the number of crimes, the times and locations.

One of Simon's most enjoyable tasks is to visit local schools to speak to young people and encourage them to be more safety aware and to deter them from being a nuisance or committing crime. Simon is measured on how effective his actions are in reducing anti-social behaviour and crimes being committed in his area of responsibility.

He has been asked to visit the local primary school to talk to a group of ten-year-olds. This is at the request of the head teacher and the parent association as there have been a series of shop lifting incidents at the local newsagents and supermarket. Some of the children are friends of the culprits and belong to their gangs. A few are in danger of committing similar crimes, thinking that this is a 'cool' thing to do. The request came by email from the head teacher so Simon made sure he responded by telephone and then by email within the response time of five days (as published on the police website). He has organised a time to speak to the children and must now prepare for the presentation.

He carries out the following tasks prior to the presentation:

- Locates the literature about the consequences of shoplifting and theft.
- Looks at the crime reporting statistics to see how many incidents of shoplifting have been committed in the last six months at the newsagents.
- Speaks to his manager (the police sergeant) about what he can and cannot put in the presentation in terms of format and content.
- Carries out research on the internet and talks to colleagues to make sure his presentation is accurate and up to date.
- Puts the presentation together using a software presentation package and rehearses it with a colleague.
- Asks for feedback from his colleague.
- Changes the presentation to include some photographs and make it more appropriate to ten-year-olds, as suggested by his colleague.

On the day, Simon:

- ensures that he conforms to his organisation's standards of appearance and health and safety by wearing the correct uniform, his personal protective equipment (i.e. protective vest, hat, footwear) and radio before he leaves the police station
- reports to the school reception and signs in to comply with his customer's health and safety requirements and asks for a visitor's badge
- safeguards the children and himself by asking a teacher to stay with him when he is presenting to the children in case of any emergencies

- makes sure that the cables from the computer and projector that he is using are not causing a hazard to the children and they do not have any liquid refreshments near the electricity source
- checks the projector screen stand has a safety catch so that it does not collapse and fall on the audience
- asks the children and teacher to speak up if they do not understand some of the information, they cannot see the projector screen or he is speaking too fast or too quietly.

After the presentation, Simon:

- asks if there are any questions
- hands out the information leaflets
- thanks the head teacher for her hospitality.

Questions

1. What could Simon have prepared and taken to the presentation to prove to his sergeant that his message to the children had made an impact?
2. Who should Simon get feedback from to check his service delivery and how should the feedback be obtained?

The reflective activity below is designed to help you to start thinking about your reactions and feelings when you encounter different customer service scenarios. We are all customers on a regular basis, so this activity is from the perspective of you as the customer. It will help to prepare you to collect evidence that will demonstrate your knowledge, understanding and practical skills in customer service. Write down your reflections if you wish as they may be useful in discussions or sessions with your assessor or in the preparation of evidence.

REFLECTIVE ACTIVITY 1

Analyse a recent experience when you were the customer buying a complex product or service, such as insurance, a computer, a mobile telephone or a holiday, or were taking a car in for servicing or repair.

1. How well had the customer service professional prepared for the transaction?
2. Did their service match the service promises made prior to the transaction via their website, letters, email promotions or advertising?
3. Were there any points in the transaction when they disappointed you or did not meet your expectations?
4. How did they check if you were satisfied with their service (formal or informal)?
5. Did you have an opportunity to provide any feedback? If yes, what did you tell them?
6. How did they react to your feedback and did they offer to take any actions or make any changes?

Performance evidence for Unit B2 (LO1, LO2 and LO3)

The tutorial, questions, case study and reflective activity have given you the opportunity to consider the customer service provided in different customer service settings and to think about delivering reliable customer service from your own perspective.

The next section in this unit is designed to help you focus on the learning outcomes and performance requirement of Unit B2 and prompt you to consider how you can evidence this through your customer service role. It is expected that the evidence that you generate for this unit will also cross-reference with some of the other units in the qualification. The virtual advisor will guide you to collect the evidence that you need to complete this unit.

Performance evidence is different from knowledge evidence and requires you to identify events that have happened in the course of your job in a real work environment. You will have to prove that the customers really exist and the events or incidents really happened – your assessor will help you to do this. The ways that you can present the evidence will be explained in Tutorials 2–5 below. You should answer the questions in the context of where you work and your provision of customer service. This time it *is* important for you to record your answers in writing as this will be the foundation of your evidence. However, you need only write notes to remind you where the proof is located.

LO1 Prepare to deal with customers

Assessment criteria

1.1 Keep their knowledge of their organisation's services or products up-to-date
1.2 Ensure that the area they work in is tidy, safe and organised efficiently
1.3 Prepare and arrange everything they need to deal with customers before their shift or period of work commences

TUTORIAL 2 with your virtual advisor:

The three assessment criteria in Unit B2 learning outcome 1 are about your up-front customer service preparation.

Much of the knowledge supporting assessment criterion 1.1 has been discussed in learning outcome 4 earlier in this chapter where you were asked to demonstrate an understanding of and describe your organisation's services or products. The research that you carry out as part of your job role will help you to evidence this criterion; in addition you can use the notes or the statement that you prepared for discussion with your assessor in answer to the questions in assessment criterion 4.1.

The best methods of evidencing assessment criteria 1.2 and 1.3 are through observation and questioning by your assessor. However, this might not always be possible so an alternative might be a planned discussion or a written statement to evidence how you ensure your area of work is safe, tidy and organised. If your assessor has not been able to see this first hand they might ask for further supporting evidence. This could come from quality audits of your workstation or area, mystery shopper reports or personal reviews where housekeeping and health and safety are assessed. They may speak to your manager or supervisor for confirmation or you might be able to request a written endorsement of your performance from them.

Performance evidence activity 1

Prepare some notes on the following so that you can carry out a conversation with your assessor.

- How you keep your knowledge of your organisation's products and services up to date.
- How you carry out general duties to keep your work area clean, tidy and safe.
- What you need to prepare and arrange before you start your shift or period of work.

What work products can you use to support the above?

LO2 Give consistent service to customers

Assessment criteria

2.1 Make realistic customer service promises to customers
2.2 Ensure that their promises balance the needs of their customers and their organisation
2.3 Keep their promises to customers
2.4 Inform their customers if they cannot keep their promises due to unforeseen circumstances
2.5 Recognise when their customers' needs or expectations have changed and adapt their service to meet the new requirements
2.6 Keep their customers informed if delivery of the service needs to involve passing them on to another person or organisation

TUTORIAL 3 with your virtual advisor:

During every customer service transaction you should only make promises that are within the limits of your responsibility or that you know can be fulfilled because they are accepted company policy (assessment criterion 2.1). They must be SMART (specific, measurable, achievable, realistic and timed). Here is an example of a SMART promise regarding the sale of a book from an online retailer:

- Specific: we can fast-track the delivery of the book at a cost of £2
- Measurable: next day delivery guaranteed
- Achievable: buy before 10a.m., goods despatched before 11 a.m. the same day
- Realistic: using a tried, tested and reliable delivery service
- Timed: delivered by lunchtime the next day.

If you are able to keep your promise it is likely your customer will be delighted; however, if you make unrealistic promises then this could damage the customer relationship. If the promise is outside of your authority then it is important that you know who to ask or where to check so that you can provide an answer to the customer. In the case study in Chapter 3 Unit A4, Liz failed to seize an opportunity to delight her customer by not checking information with her head office, her manager or on the internet. In addition, she failed to provide the reasoning behind her decision and because of this she disappointed her customer. This incident will have a long-lasting effect on the customer and their confidence in the organisation could be damaged.

Assessment criteria 2.2, 2.3 and 2.4 refer to the need to think carefully about any promises that are made to customers. There can be times when the promise that you make to the customer is weighted heavily in their favour in order to meet their needs, maintain their satisfaction and retain their loyalty. If it is a promise that you have made alone you need to judge whether it will be cost-effective to the organisation in the short- or long-term. You also need to identify the possible effects if you do not meet the customer's requirements. You need to know who to go to for advice and guidance if you do not have the authority, confidence or understanding to make the decision alone. Often a manager or more experienced colleague will be able to see the overall impact that keeping the promise will have on the organisation and the customer.

To put this in context we will revisit the example of a customer purchasing a book from an online retailer:

- The customer wants the book delivered the next day to arrive by midday. However, it is now two in the afternoon and the customer has missed the guaranteed delivery promise deadline. The customer telephones the customer service helpline and asks if the book can be despatched immediately and still get to them by midday tomorrow. The customer service professional wants to provide excellent service; he can see from their purchasing history they are a regular customer and they are local. He offers to deliver the book on his way home and the customer is delighted by the offer. The transaction is completed and the promise made.

- When the customer service professional goes to the despatch department to collect the book the despatch supervisor explains that there is no procedure for collections and the book has already gone out on the normal delivery schedule and will not arrive until the day after tomorrow.

This is an example of an unachievable promise made in good faith, but which does not balance with the needs of the organisation; the result will be a disappointed customer.

Questions

1. What action should the customer service professional have taken before making the promise?

2. What action will the customer service professional have to take now?

In some cases promises will be affected by circumstances beyond anyone's control (for example adverse weather, transport problems) and in these situations it will be necessary to take action to inform the customer. The way in which this is communicated will depend on the resources available to you, but it is important to remember the rules of good communication and to use the method that will cause the least confusion and distress.

To meet the requirements of assessment criteria 2.5 and 2.6 you need to recognise that good customer service involves being one step ahead of the customer whenever possible and reading signs and signals that indicate a change in needs or expectations. Let us now look at the example of Mary.

- Mary has banked with Fast Interest bank for many years and has used lots of their banking services. She recently inherited some money and wanted to invest it in an ISA (individual savings account) she already held but could not seem to do this via the bank's internet service. She visited her local branch of the bank and asked for advice at the customer service desk.

- The advisor, Jean, explained that it was not possible to carry out this type of transaction online. She took Mary's details and looked at her banking history. She made a quick assessment of the situation and knowing and understanding the products and services that Fast Interest offered, she identified and explained in detail to Mary that she could make some changes to her existing accounts and get a better rate of return on her money. She also arranged for her to have the inheritance paid into a new ISA but informed her that she had to pass this to a colleague in another department, James. She arranged an appointment for Mary to meet James who would complete all the legal paperwork with her for HMRC (Her Majesty's Revenue and Customs).

- Had she not visited the branch Mary would not have known about the products or understood how she could get a better rate. She left the bank feeling satisfied that her needs had been met and that her money was safely invested.

Question

1. Describe an occasion when you have identified a change in the needs of your customer and adapted your services to meet the new requirements. Write this down in a statement or prepare some notes to discuss with your assessor

Performance evidence activity 2

Provide four examples of promises that you have made to customers. Try to vary the examples to show when you have delivered reliable service during routine, busy and quiet times and when people, systems or resources have let you down.

1. One example should show how you had to balance the needs of the customer and the organisation. How did you make sure that the promises were not unrealistic and were not outside the accepted procedures of your organisation?

2. Another example should show where you had to explain to the customer that the promise could not be met due to unforeseen circumstances.

3. A third example should demonstrate how you referred the customer to another person in the organisation and explain how you informed the customer.

4. The final example should evidence a time when you had to get advice from a manager or colleague because you could not meet the expectations of the customer on your own authority.

Make some notes of each incident in preparation for a discussion, or write a short statement supported by a witness statement or work products. Remember that some customer information might be confidential so always be aware of data protection when producing your evidence.

LO3 Check customer service delivery

Assessment criteria

3.1 Check that the service they have given meets their customers' needs and expectations

3.2 Identify when they could have given better service to customers and how their service could have been improved

3.3 Share information with colleagues and service partners to maintain and improve their standards of service delivery

TUTORIAL 4 with your virtual advisor:

In Tutorial 1, assessment criteria 4.3 and 4.4, you looked at the methods or systems in place to measure and check service delivery. In learning outcome 3 you will need to evidence how you check that you have met your customer's needs and expectations, how you analyse what you could have done better and how you share that information with colleagues and others to maintain and improve the services.

You will need:

- to identify the ways that you collect feedback from customers, both formal and informal

- to show that you have reviewed the feedback so that you can identify patterns and trends and identify where improvements can be made. This might be in meetings with colleagues and service partners, one-to-ones with your manager or supervisor or informal chats with others.

Performance evidence activity 3

In Tutorial 1 you were asked to list all the feedback systems used in your organisation; you now need to expand on these.

1. Describe a scenario where you have collected feedback from your customer in an informal way.
   - How did you do this?
   - What did this feedback tell you?
   - Who did you share this with?
   - How did you make improvements to the products or services provided?

2. Explain how you have been involved in collecting formal feedback from your customers.
   - Who asked you to collect the feedback?
   - How was this done?
   - Who analysed the feedback?
   - How was this information shared with colleagues and service partners?
   - What improvements were made as a result of this feedback?

Once again, you will find it very useful to make notes that you can later share with your assessor in a discussion. You might want to collect some examples of the feedback systems used (questionnaires, customer suggestions, emails) to support your notes. This will provide the foundation to your evidence for this learning outcome. The performance activities you have been asked to complete will help you to pull all of the preparation together and show your evidence through some 'live' examples of customer service transactions. Your explanation can be used in final evidence but will need to be endorsed or supported by witnesses or work products.

TUTORIAL 5 with your virtual advisor:

Evidence requirements provide the context in which you meet the assessment criteria for performance and enable your assessor to judge whether you are competent in a number of different situations. You do not need to cover the evidence requirements separately; they will be covered as you complete the assessment criteria. Your assessor will give you guidance. The evidence requirements for Unit B2 are explained below:

● *You must provide evidence that you have worked with different customers who have different needs and expectations.* In Chapter 1 Unit F1 (learning outcome 1 and assessment criterion 3.3) and Chapter 4 Unit A10 (assessment criterion 3.8) you examined the different types of customers that you deal with and how to identify their needs and expectations. To meet this evidence requirement you will need to present examples of customer interactions, over a period of time, that show that you have dealt with a range of different customers, such as vulnerable people, demanding customers and customers familiar with your products and services.

● *You must provide evidence of delivering reliable customer service during routine delivery of customer service.* This is when you are working in normal circumstances, not under extra pressure or dealing with unusual circumstances like holiday periods or seasonal surges (such as national holidays). You need to establish what is normal!

● *You must provide evidence of delivering reliable customer service during a busy time in your job.* Once you have decided on the routine delivery of customer service, you will be able to identify your busy times. Quite often you are aware of the times when you are busy and you can take this into consideration when selecting opportunities for your evidence collection.

● *You must provide evidence of delivering reliable customer service during a quiet time in your job.* In the same way you have identified a busy time in your job, you can now identify when it is a quiet time. Maybe you have examples of how you had a meeting to discuss the delivery of reliable customer service during a quiet period, or you used the time to gather some feedback from your customers.

● *You must provide evidence of delivering reliable customer service when people, systems or resources have let you down.* This might be a situation beyond your control, for example, the stock that you were expecting and promised to a customer arrives damaged, or a promise to call a customer back by a certain time, made by you, is not followed through by your colleague who has taken over the transaction. You need to be able demonstrate how you still manage to maintain reliable customer service throughout this adversity.

Performance evidence activity 4 will help you to pull all of the preparation together and show your evidence through some 'live' examples of customer service transactions. Your explanation can be used in final evidence but will need to be endorsed or supported by witnesses or work products.

Performance evidence activity 4

To help with planning your evidence, make some notes about some situations you have experienced. You should provide examples of delivering reliable customer service (one for each context) during:

- a quiet time in your job.
- when people, systems or resources have let you down
- routine delivery of customer service
- a busy time in your job.

Try to incorporate an example of dealing with different customer needs and expectations in each transaction. You might find that you have already prepared some examples from other activities in this or other chapters. It is acceptable to use these examples as it will provide you with experience of cross-referencing your evidence; your assessor should be able to support you with this concept.

LEARNER EVALUATION ACTIVITY

The last activity is the learner evaluation. Each section in this chapter is intended to help you to develop yourself towards being a more thinking and reflective customer service professional. The learner evaluation requires you to reflect on your learning from completing this unit guide. Once again, this does not have to be written; however, it could be useful to record your answers for use in reviews with your line manager, supervisor, assessor, tutor or possibly in a job interview.

Documenting your learning throughout your working life is an effective way of showing that you use experience to influence your performance and behaviours. Reflect on what you knew at the start of the unit and what you know now.

1. What have you learned from completing this unit?
2. Identify three phrases that were new to you.
3. How will completing this unit impact on your customer service within your organisation?
4. Highlight an improvement that you have made as a result of completing the unit.

If you are working towards Unit D3 Develop personal performance through delivering customer service, your evaluations might provide you with some foundation evidence.

Summary

This concludes the unit guidance for Unit B2 Deliver reliable customer service.

You should be prepared to submit evidence for both the knowledge and performance aspects of the unit learning outcomes:

LO1: Prepare to deal with customers
LO2: Give consistent service to customers
LO3: Check customer service delivery
LO4: Know how to deliver reliable customer service

You will now be able to describe how you deliver reliable customer service through effective preparation, by making realistic promises to your customer and by actively seeking and using feedback to improve the service provided.

It is likely that the knowledge and performance evidence you produce for this unit will cross-reference to the following Customer Service units:

- Unit A4 Give customers a positive impression of yourself and your organisation
- Unit A10 Dealing with customers face to face
- Unit A11 Deal with incoming telephone calls from customers
- Unit C1 Recognise and deal with customer queries requests and problems
- Unit D1 Develop customer relationships
- Unit F1 Communicate using customer service language.

RECOGNISE AND DEAL WITH CUSTOMER QUERIES, REQUESTS AND PROBLEMS

Learning outcomes

Learning outcomes for Unit C1:

1. Recognise and deal with customer queries and requests

2. Recognise and deal with customer problems

3. Know how to recognise and deal with customer queries, requests and problems

This unit guide is a resource to help you gather the evidence that you require to achieve Unit C1, one of the optional units in the 'Handling problems' theme of the Level 2 NVQ Certificate in Customer Service. It can be used as a learning resource if you are new to your role, are studying customer service in preparation for work or as a refresher if you are an experienced customer service professional.

Recognise and deal with customer queries, requests and problems – what is Unit C1 about?

No matter how good you are at providing consistent and reliable customer service, some of your customers will from time to time expect more. They can signal this in various ways and when they do you must know how to handle the situation. Sometimes customers ask different questions and request special treatment. You may be able to help them and they certainly need to know who to ask for help if necessary. Some customers may be dissatisfied with the service and may present a problem. Your job is to recognise that there is a problem and make sure that the appropriate person deals with it.

Source: Adapted from Unit B2 purpose and aim

You will be required to demonstrate how to recognise customer queries, requests and how to seek help from colleagues if you cannot deal with the issue on your own. You will demonstrate how you deal with problems in a number of different contexts over a sufficient period of time and how you recognise when to hand the problem over to others in the organisation. You should also be able to identify and explain who is who in your organisation, how to deal with difficult people and situations, and the procedures in your organisation for dealing with problems, including complaints.

Completing this unit guide

To complete this unit guide you will need to:

1. Read through the information in each section.
2. Look at the case study and reflective activity and use the questions to help you to test your understanding.

There is no set format for working through or recording your answers in these sections, just use them in a way that suits your learning style, unless otherwise instructed by your assessor or tutor. The case study and reflective activity are linked to the assessment criteria in learning outcome 3, which focuses on the underpinning knowledge and understanding for Unit C1. Learning outcome 3 has been presented first so that you understand the background to the criteria in learning outcomes 1 and 2. If you work through this section first you will find that your performance evidence will be easier to identify and present to your assessor.

Learning outcome 3 – Knowledge evidence

LO3 Know how to recognise and deal with customer queries, requests and problems

- The tutorial section is designed to explain the assessment criteria. In this section your virtual advisor will provide you with information to help you interpret the national standards.

- The case study and reflective activity will help you to prepare to discuss and explain your understanding of customer service with your assessor.

Learning outcomes 1 and 2 – Performance evidence

LO1 Recognise and deal with customer queries and requests
LO2 Recognise and deal with customer problems

In addition to the learning outcomes, in this unit there are performance **evidence requirements** that indicate the circumstances or conditions under which you should present the evidence.

Your evidence must include examples of problems which are:

- brought to your attention by customers
- identified first by you and/or by your colleagues.

The problems included in your evidence must include examples of:

- a difference between customer expectations and what is offered by your organisation
- a problem resulting from a system or procedure failure.

Why do I need to recognise and deal with customer queries, requests and problems?

Customer service is not just a job; it underpins everything you do in your work role. If you are involved in providing products or services to others, internal or external to your organisation, it is essential that you are able to:

- identify when your customers need more information or clarification or have requests and questions about the products or services you provide and that you address those requirements
- deal with problems when they occur and identify when it is appropriate to involve others in finding a solution.

The cycle of recognising requests, queries and problems

This unit is about recognising and taking appropriate action when dealing with customers when they come to you to request additional information, question you about a product or service or have a problem. It is important to recognise the difference between a:

- request: to ask for, demand, call for …
- query: an enquiry, a doubt, uncertainty, a question …
- problem: a difficulty, crisis, dilemma, setback or obstacle …

The cycle of recognising requests, queries and problems illustrates four important stages of problem recognition.

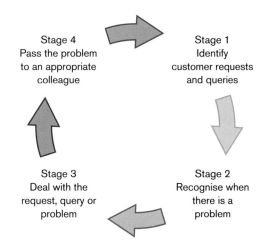

Figure C1.1: The cycle of recognising requests, queries and problems

Stage 1 Identify customer requests and queries

During a transaction it is expected that you will know what you want or have to say to a customer. You will also recognise typical reactions from your customer (i.e. what they say and how they say it, as well as their body language or facial expressions) and have supplementary information that you are able to supply. This situation can be easy to address but you may sometimes get a request that you have not encountered before; the customer might ask you to make an exception to the service you normally provide or they might want extra information that you have not prepared. Similarly, the customer might have a question or query that you are unprepared for. In both cases the request or query should not be seen as an intrusion or a problem.

Stage 2 Recognise when there is a problem

Stage 2 involves recognising that there is a problem. The problem could be identified by you or it could be raised by the customer. In the latter case, you will be able to recognise there is something amiss from what the customer is saying as well as their tone of voice, body language and facial expression. As a customer service professional it is vital that you appreciate the problem from the customer's point of view.

Stage 3 Deal with the request, query or problem

At this stage it is important for you to listen and act in response to the query, request or problem. You need to use your communication skills and deal with the situation in a calm and confident manner and recognise when the request, query or problem is too much for you to handle. You need to have a good understanding of your company policies and procedures for handling complaints or making exceptions to normal standards of customer service.

Stage 4 Pass the problem to an appropriate colleague

If you realise that you cannot make a decision or a request is outside of your area of authority or experience, then you need to seek help and advice from a colleague. You need to know who will be most able to assist you, what they can do and where they are located.

Each time you go through this cycle of events with a customer you will learn to pick up on new signs and signals and also increase your knowledge of who, in your organisation, can help in different situations. Eventually your knowledge will increase so that you have to ask less and will be able to make independent decisions with confidence.

Knowledge evidence for Unit C1 (LO3)

As stated earlier, we are starting with learning outcome 3 (LO3). This contains the knowledge criteria for the unit. In order to sustain and improve in your role as a customer service professional it is essential that you have this knowledge to underpin your performance. The criteria in LO3 have been grouped into common themes; they are therefore not in number sequence.

LO3 Know how to recognise and deal with customer queries, requests and problems

Assessment criteria

3.1   List who in the organisation is able to give help and information
3.2   State the limits of what they are allowed to do
3.3   Identify what professional behaviour is
3.4   Describe how to speak to people who are dissatisfied
3.5   Describe how to deal with difficult people
3.6   State what customers normally expect
3.7   Identify how to recognise a problem from what a customer says or does
3.8   Describe what kinds of behaviours/actions would make situations worse
3.9   List the organisational procedures they must follow when they deal with problems or complaints
3.10 Identify the types of behaviour that may make a problem worse

TUTORIAL 1 with your virtual advisor:

Read through this tutorial so that you can meet the requirements of the assessment criteria shown above.

3.1 List who in the organisation is able to give help and information

In Chapter 1 Unit F1 Tutorial 1, we looked at how you identify who's who and who does what to deliver customer service in your organisation. You were asked to explain how to find information about your organisation's services and products. All of these activities are closely linked to this criterion, where you are asked to identify and list people who can provide help and information to you within your organisation. This information should be readily available to you through training meetings, networking and team activities.

You will need to show your assessor a list of those you can go to or call on if you need help or advice. You can make notes in preparation for a discussion or you can put the list into a personal statement. You can also refer to evidence you gathered for assessment criteria 3.11 and 3.13 from Chapter 1 Unit F1.

3.2 State the limits of what they are allowed to do

When you started your job you should have been informed about your role and responsibilities. You should also have been given information on the limits of your responsibilities. Many organisations provide their employees with a job description or a role profile explaining the extent of their role. If you have been given a job induction it is possible the limits of what you are allowed to do may have been explained to you. If you do not know, then you need to ask, especially if your role has legal implications, for example, providing confidential information, using machinery or serving alcohol. If you break the law or your organisation's guidelines you could be disciplined for the offence.

Question

1. In the context of responding to requests, queries and problems explain the limits of what you are able to do in your role. Your answer can be in note form in preparation for a discussion with your assessor or a personal statement.

3.3 Identify what professional behaviour is

Chapter 3 Unit A4, learning outcome 4 is all about understanding how to give customers a positive impression of yourself and your organisation. We discussed standards of appearance and what is seen as acceptable in an organisation. Professional behaviour is vital in any organisation even if there is a relaxed or casual approach to customer service. Standards of behaviour and language will vary depending on the customer base; what is deemed acceptable with internal customers might need to be adjusted when dealing with external customers.

Professional behaviour in any business context needs to be kept in line with legal obligations and decency. Employers do not allow their employees to swear or to treat others face to face, verbally or in writing in an offensive manner.

It is also important to find out how customers should be addressed and this might vary from customer to customer. It may be perfectly acceptable to refer to an internal customer by their first name, but the approach to external customers might be much more formal and you may be required to call them 'Sir' or 'Madam'. The important factor is that you find out what your organisation's protocol is.

An organisation's rules relating to professional behaviour might also extend to:

- friendships with customers outside of work
- eating, drinking and smoking while on duty
- use of company facilities such as the computer
- appropriate dress codes.

Questions

1. Identify what professional behaviour means to you within your organisation. Speak to a manager or experienced colleague and list some of the standards you have to comply with.

2. Speak to a friend or family member and ask them what professional behaviour means to them in their organisation. What standards of professional behaviour do they have to meet?

Make some notes so that you can discuss this with your assessor, or write a personal statement to identify what professional behaviour is applicable to you.

3.4 Describe how to speak to people who are dissatisfied
3.5 Describe how to deal with difficult people
3.7 Identify how to recognise a problem from what a customer says or does

3.10 Identify the types of behaviour that may make a problem worse

The above criteria have been clustered together because they all relate to dealing with customers who have a problem at some point in the customer service transaction. This may or may not be a problem in reality, however, it is important to recognise the state of the customer's emotions and react in the correct way.

What is a problem? It can be defined as a difficult situation, matter or person, a question that needs to be solved or a setback. To put into context, it could be faulty goods, a failed customer promise, breach of contract or unacceptable behaviour.

When a customer complains because they have a problem or they are dissatisfied it has taken them time and effort to do so, so they will want a resolution. The most important thing is to recognise the importance they place on the problem. If you do not take the problem seriously, mock it or dismiss it without being seen to take action you will inflame the situation.

Before you can recognise when a customer is dissatisfied, unhappy or is going to be a challenge, you need to understand and recognise what they want and need from you. You need to have a basic understanding of human behaviour and be able to identify emotions in yourself and others; this is known as emotional intelligence. In Tutorial 2, Chapter 3 Unit A4, we looked at how current and past experiences can influence the way we react to the behaviour of others in the context of how to recognise when a customer is angry or confused. You can also apply this information to this criterion. Remember, an adverse reaction from a customer service professional, in terms of negative behaviour or body language, could make a situation worse.

In Chapter 3 we looked at how to recognise and respond appropriately to what a customer wants. Here, in assessment criterion 3.4, you are being asked to take this one step further by describing how you speak to people who you have recognised are dissatisfied and who may therefore be difficult to handle. You will have interpreted their dissatisfaction by listening carefully to their vocabulary and pitch and tone of voice and perhaps observation of their body language and facial expression. In terms of what you say, your response should be professional and calm; choose your words carefully and avoid using phrases that could make the situation worse, for example, 'that was a stupid thing to do' or 'why didn't you let us know before?' Do not swear or use language that could be interpreted as insensitive or appear negative or uncaring. Assertiveness can be a very useful behaviour for a customer service professional when dealing with a difficult or dissatisfied customer. Assertiveness is about using clear and direct communication; feelings, particularly anger, are kept under control and are expressed in a straightforward manner which takes into account the feelings and opinions of others. Being assertive involves talking through what can be achieved in a reasoned manner.

It might be helpful to take some time to observe situations at work or when you are a customer to look at the way that two people talk and react in a situation when one person is dissatisfied. There will be good and bad examples and you can use these to help you to prepare notes for this knowledge evidence.

Questions

Prepare some written notes explaining how you:

● recognise a problem from what a customer says or does

● deal with difficult or challenging people

● speak to people who are dissatisfied

● identify the types of behaviour that may make a problem worse.

Your notes will form the basis of a personal statement or provide guidance if you have a discussion with your assessor.

Figure C1.2

3.6 State what customers normally expect

You need to know what your organisation promises to its customers in terms of products, services, conditions, after-care, service levels, contracts and agreements. We looked at this in detail in Chapter 1 Unit F1 when you were asked to identify your organisation's service offer and the products and services it offers. If these are published via advertising, the internet, customer charters, mission statements and service level agreements, then this will be the minimum that your customer expects. However, with increased competition and aggressive advertising you might find your customer expects your organisation to offer them the same as your competitors. In order to be prepared for this, you should carry out some research into what your competitors are offering.

Question

1. Make a list of the promises or minimum service levels a customer will expect from you.

3.9 List the organisational procedures they must follow when they deal with problems or complaints

It is vital that you have an awareness of the complaints or appeals processes that exist in your organisation. Some of these will be based on legal requirements, for instance a complaints procedure in a retailer will be based on the laws relating to the sale of goods and services. In the financial sector a customer must be told about the complaints procedure which might involve an external regulator. This is often explained to a customer by the customer service professional over the telephone or in the small print on forms and information leaflets. Although the customer might not remember what they are told, you must make sure you know how your organisation's complaints procedure works and use it correctly when necessary.

3.8 Describe what kinds of behaviours/actions would make situations worse

To evidence this assessment criterion you need to think back to what your customers expect and what your organisation promises to them.

The kinds of behaviours and actions that make a situation worse are when the standards and promises do not meet the customer's expectations or the customer service professional acts in an unprofessional way.

A customer expects to be treated in a friendly and polite way and to be provided with information, products and services that suit their needs. If these needs are not met they will become unhappy, dissatisfied, confused and angry. If a customer service professional does not fulfil their promises, or provides incorrect or inconsistent information this is likely to lead to further disharmony.

The types of behaviour that will irritate a customer are lack of understanding (about the customer's situation and the impact it has on their life), rudeness, disinterest, inappropriate comments, patronising attitude, failure to update information, failure to meet deadlines and not being listened to. The problem the customer has is really important to them at that moment in time. If it is not resolved the situation will escalate and you might not be able to retrieve it, resulting in a loss of business and negative publicity. Remember: customers have the power to tell others about their bad experiences within a few seconds through the use of social networking and internet feedback.

The case study section provides an opportunity for you to read about a customer service scenario and consolidates some of the information from the tutorial. You can use this to reflect on the situation and answer some questions. Once again you do not have to write your answers down unless your tutor or assessor has asked you to do so.

CASE STUDY 1: The chain reaction

The sequence of events following a car accident is shown below. It illustrates the different types of communication methods used in the various customer service transactions and what can go wrong.

1. Ivor Dent has a car accident and exchanges details <u>in writing</u> with the other (third) party.

2. Ivor <u>telephones</u> Windruffs of Portsmouth (the car dealership where he purchased the car) and requests that they check the car for internal damage.

3. Mary Jones, customer service desk executive at Windruffs, arranges for Ivor to bring the car in. Mary books the date and time with Ivor and records this <u>in writing</u> on the computer.

4. John Smith, responsible for insurance claims liaison at Windruffs, picks up <u>the email</u> from Mary and replies to Ivor <u>by phone</u>.

5. Ivor comes into Windruffs. John meets him <u>face to face</u> and takes the details <u>in writing</u> of the accident and <u>photos</u> of the car damage.

6. John Smith communicates <u>face to face</u> that the Windruffs's service offer promises that he can have a courtesy car, delivered at a time of his choice and to his home, on the day his car goes in for repair. He gives Ivor a <u>written</u> copy of this promise. John assures Ivor that he will hear directly from the insurance company, B&S Insurance, acting on Windruffs's behalf.

7. John processes the incident <u>in writing</u> on the Windruffs database and sends an <u>email</u> with the attached records to B&S Insurance.

8. Amy at B&S Insurance receives <u>the email</u> and makes a <u>telephone</u> call to John to check the details and to tell him they will start the claim process.

9. Amy <u>updates her database</u> with additional information and <u>telephones</u> Ivor to reassure him that all is in hand.

10. Amy contacts Ivor's insurers and the third party's insurers <u>by telephone</u> to check all insurances are up to date.

11. Amy updates her records <u>in writing</u>.

12. Amy contacts Ivor <u>by text</u> on his mobile to let him know all is going ahead.

13. Amy needs further details of the accident for her records. She <u>telephones</u> Ivor and asks him to draw a diagram of the accident and the time and weather conditions.

14. Ivor puts this <u>in writing</u> and posts it to Amy.

15. Amy contacts the third party's insurers <u>by telephone</u> to get the same information.

16. Amy <u>collates and records</u> all information on her system when she has this returned to her.

17. Amy has enough information to let Windruffs know they can go ahead with the repair and the courtesy car will be paid for on insurance so she sends <u>an email</u> to them.

18. Amy goes on holiday so she asks Ben to take the case over. She speaks to him <u>face to face</u> and gives him <u>written</u> hand over notes in an <u>email</u>.

19. Ben contacts Ivor <u>by phone</u> to arrange the date for the courtesy car to be delivered.

20. When the date is arranged, Ben <u>emails</u> Ivor's details to Best Cars Hire Car company (who will supply the courtesy car), the address to drop the hire car off and details of where to take Ivor's car for repair. He copies the details into the email from the B&S database.

21. Mary at Best Cars picks up the email and <u>types</u> the details into their system.

22. The information is recorded on the <u>weekly jobs list print out</u> and collected by Fred, the manager, at the Plymouth depot. He allocates the car drop-off to Charlie and puts the <u>printed paperwork</u> from the Best Cars system in Charlie's to-do tray.

23. The night before the drop-off Charlie picks up <u>the paperwork</u> and reads where he is going and what time Ivor is expecting him (by 8.30 a.m.).

24. Charlie speaks to Fred <u>face to face</u> because he is puzzled why he is dropping a car off in Plymouth and picking up the damaged car and is driving it to Portsmouth for repair. Fred agrees it is odd but says that he should do as instructed.

25. Charlie <u>telephones</u> Ivor at 7.30 a.m. on the day of the drop-off because he cannot find Ivor's address in Plymouth on his satellite navigation system or on the street map. Ivor asks where Charlie is calling from. He says he is in Plymouth. Ivor explains his home is in Portsmouth. Charlie explains that he is three hours' driving time away so he will be with Ivor as quickly as he can. Ivor is concerned because he has a business appointment at 10.00 a.m. and will have to cancel it.

26. Ivor has to <u>phone</u> his customer to cancel his business appointment and is told that he cannot rearrange his appointment. He has lost his business opportunity and the contract.

27. Charlie arrives at Ivor's home by 10.30 a.m. He is met by a very angry Ivor and he apologises again, checks the car details and swaps the cars. They establish that Charlie's <u>paperwork</u> has the wrong postcode.

28. Ivor is satisfied with Charlie's service and that of Windruffs but is confused and wants to know where this went wrong. He <u>phones</u> Amy at B&S Insurance. She listens to his problem but she is not very helpful and laughs it off and says, 'Well, you have the car now and it's worth more and is a better model than your own car, so you should be happy'.

29. Ivor is angry at the loss of his contract and Amy's reaction and when a questionnaire comes from B&S Insurance about the customer experience he records his dissatisfaction <u>in writing</u>. He hears nothing further from B&S Insurance.

30. Ivor's car is repaired at Meads Repair Shop and he is <u>telephoned</u> by Susan when it is ready.

31. Ivor drops the car back to Meads and meets Susan <u>face to face</u>, who signs off the paperwork and hands over his repaired car. He is happy with the standard of repair and the convenience of the courtesy car but still angry and unhappy about the problem with the drop-off as he lost a contract worth £3000. This has been an expensive free service!

32. Ivor takes his car in for its annual service to Windruffs a couple of weeks later. He is still angry because he has had no response to his feedback to B&S Insurance. He explains, <u>face to face</u>, the incident and its consequences to Mike, the customer complaints executive at Windruffs. Mike listens and Ivor asks him to formally record the error. Mike assures him that he will pass this on.

33. Ivor hears nothing and then receives a customer service questionnaire from Windruffs. He has the option to complete a <u>paper copy</u> or electronically on <u>the website</u>. They ask him to rate the service he has received in the last two weeks. He completes the paper version and rates some areas of Windruffs' service highly but his experience and the lack of response to his dissatisfaction has spoilt his overall rating of the organisation. Once again he provides additional comments about the incident. He just wants an apology!

34. Ivor is so incensed about the lack of reaction from B&S Insurance and Windruffs that he decides to use his social networking site to write about his experiences in a less than favourable light. He has over 200 followers on his site.

35. Ivor is still waiting for an apology. He is so disappointed with the lack of response from Windruffs and B&S Insurance that he has decided not to use either organisation again in the future.

As you can see, there are many people involved in this customer service transaction and many communication methods. One small, almost insignificant error can affect the customer's overall experience, cause a problem and damage their loyalty to an organisation, not to mention the number of people that then get to hear their story!

Questions

1. At what point during the transaction did things start to go wrong?

2. Who could have prevented this from happening?

3. Make a list of the behaviours/actions (or lack of) that made the situation worse.

4. What action could staff at B&S Insurance and Windruffs have taken to change Ivor's overall perception of the experience?

TUTORIAL 2 with your virtual advisor:

Read through this tutorial so that you can meet the requirements of the assessment criteria shown above.

When a customer wants to access a service or purchase a product they will either require information from you to help them make an informed choice, or they will have carried out some research prior to the transaction. They may have looked at your organisation's customer promise or the terms and conditions of the contract and they will have certain expectations. They may have booked something using the internet in the belief that this would be the simplest course of action, but then found that the online system or process gave them problems. Or, as in the case study above, the customer might have been promised a service over and above their expectations, only to have a small error turn it into a negative experience. This was the moment of truth!

If a customer's expectations are not met (whether they are realistic or not) they will become dissatisfied and/or angry. If you are not able to explain why they cannot be met or provide a compromise this will compound the anger or confusion. This is what happened in the case study above: Amy failed to recognise that the error had cost Ivor £3000 and he was disappointed that things had gone wrong. When she did not offer any explanation about who was responsible or offer to find out, this made it worse. Mike at Windruffs appeared to be listening but when nothing happened Ivor was again disappointed. Both B&S Insurance and Windruffs asked for customer feedback but did not act on it when it was received, so Ivor again felt let down and angry. In this case, an explanation and apology or, even better, a goodwill gesture from Windruffs or B&S Insurance might have influenced Ivor's feelings about both organisations.

The reflective activity below is designed to help you to start thinking about your reactions and feelings when you have encountered different customer service scenarios. This activity will help to prepare you to collect evidence that will demonstrate your knowledge, understanding and practical skills in customer service. Write down your reflections if you wish as they might be useful in discussions or sessions with your assessor or in the preparation of your evidence.

REFLECTIVE ACTIVITY 1

Analyse a recent transaction when you were the customer and you were dissatisfied with the products or service that you received.

1. What were you expecting before the transaction occurred, for example, because of customer promises, an advert or promotion or product/service reputation?

2. What went wrong?

3. How did the customer service professional recognise and deal with your dissatisfaction?

4. What was the final outcome?

If you have no personal transaction to refer to, talk to a friend, family member or colleague and ask them about their experience.

5. How would you have handled this situation if you had been the customer service professional?

Performance evidence for Unit C1 (LO1 and LO2)

The tutorial questions, case study and reflective activity have given you the opportunity to consider the need to recognise and deal with customer queries, requests and problems and how to share this information with others in your organisation.

The next section in this unit is designed to help you focus on the learning outcomes and performance requirements of Unit C1 and to prompt you to think how you can evidence this through your customer service role. It is expected that the evidence that you generate for this unit will also cross-reference with some of the other units in the qualification. The virtual advisor will guide you to collect the evidence that you need to complete this unit.

Performance evidence is different from knowledge evidence and requires you to identify events that have happened in the course of your job in a real work environment. You will have to prove that the customers really exist and the events or incidents really happened – your assessor will help you to do this. The ways that you can present the evidence will be explained in Tutorial 3. You should answer the questions in the context of where you work and your provision of customer service. This time it *is* important for you to record your answers in writing as this will be the foundation of your evidence. However, you need only write notes to remind you where the proof is located.

LO1 Recognise and deal with customer queries and requests

Assessment criteria

1.1 Know how to recognise and deal with customer queries, requests and problems
1.2 Seek information or help from a colleague if they cannot answer their customer's query or request
1.3 Obtain help from a colleague if they are not able to deal with their customer's request
1.4 Always tell their customer what is happening

TUTORIAL 3 with your virtual advisor:

In learning outcome 3 you looked at the knowledge criteria that demonstrate that you understand how to deal with customer queries, requests and problems. At some point during your job induction and training, or at meetings, you should have discussed with your manager and colleagues the types of queries and questions you might receive from customers and how to deal with them. As a result of discussions and experience, you will have developed an understanding of how to recognise your customers' reactions from their body language, comments and tone of voice.

You will need to provide performance evidence of how you have managed situations when you have had:

- requests for information
- questions about products and services
- problems where you have been expected to take action.

You will need some examples of transactions where you have had to ask a colleague to help you out and will also need to show that you have requested help from others when the problem was outside your area of authority or current knowledge and understanding.

Figure C1.3: Ask a colleague to help you out

Assessment criterion 1.4 requires you to always tell the customer what is happening. You will need to provide evidence that you keep your customer up to date through the most appropriate methods of communication. The best methods of evidencing these assessment criteria are through observation and questioning by your assessor. However, this might not always be possible so an alternative might be a discussion or a written statement to evidence how you recognise and deal with queries, requests and problems. You might already have made some notes from the activities in learning outcome 3, earlier in this chapter, which will help you with your discussion or question sessions.

The following tutorials and activities will help you to pull all of the preparation together and show your evidence through some 'live' examples of customer service transactions. Your explanation can be used in final evidence but will need to be endorsed or supported by witnesses or work products.

Performance evidence activity 1

To help with the planning of the observation or discussion with your assessor, make some notes about four situations you have experienced, where you have responded to the following:

1. A request from a customer that you have dealt with on your own.

2. A query from a customer that you have dealt with on your own.

3. A query when you had to ask a colleague for help or information.

4. A request which you could not deal with and had to seek help from a colleague.

LO2 Recognise and deal with customer problems

Assessment criteria
2.1 Recognise when something is a problem from the customer's point of view
2.2 Avoid saying or doing anything which may make the problem worse
2.3 Deal with a difficult customer calmly and confidently
2.4 Recognise when to pass a problem on to an appropriate colleague
2.5 Pass the problem on to their colleague with the appropriate information
2.6 Check that the customer knows what is happening

TUTORIAL 4 with your virtual advisor:

You have evidenced how you deal with requests and queries from customers in learning outcome 1; you now need to provide evidence of how you recognise and deal with customer problems. This should include problems that you can deal with alone and problems that you have to pass on to a colleague. It is important that when you pass a problem on to your colleague you provide all the information that you have available so that they can provide a complete solution.

You have looked at the knowledge that you need to support the criteria in learning outcome 3 and you now need to present your work-related performance evidence. The criteria in learning outcome 2 are best evidenced through observation and questioning, so that your assessor can see you working and interacting with your customers and colleagues. However, a personal statement about your experiences, supported by emails or a witness statement from a manager or colleague is also acceptable.

Performance evidence activity 2

To evidence the assessment criteria in learning outcome 2 you will need to identify:

- A problem that you were able to deal with on your own.
- A problem you had to pass to a colleague.

Try to include an example of each of the above. At least one of the situations should be when your customer identified a problem caused by systems or procedure failures.

- Make some notes of each incident in preparation for a planned discussion, or write a short statement supported by a witness statement or work products. Remember that some customer information might be confidential so always be aware of data protection when producing your evidence.

TUTORIAL 5 with your virtual advisor:

Evidence requirements provide the context in which you meet the assessment criteria for performance and will enable your assessor to judge whether you are competent in a number of different situations. You do not need to cover the evidence requirements separately; they will be covered as you complete the assessment criteria. Your assessor will give you guidance. The evidence requirements for Unit C1 are explained below:

- *Your evidence must include examples of problems which are brought to your attention by customers.* This could be as a result of a customer service satisfaction feedback questionnaire or through a complaint or request for a refund.

- *Your evidence must include examples of problems which are identified first by you and/or by your colleagues.* For example, you identify that the customer wanted to be contacted in writing with information, but their address (postal or email) is incomplete. You might notice that some stock that is being delivered to the customer is damaged and you will need to re-order, causing a delay in the customer's receipt of the goods.

- *The problems included in your evidence must include examples of a difference between customer expectations and what is offered by your organisation.* For example, the customer had seen the product advertised (i.e. promised) at a lower price than the price they are charged, or there was a free gift available, and this has not been included in the transaction with your organisation.

- *The problems included in your evidence must include examples of a problem resulting from a system or procedure failure.* We have looked at examples of this evidence requirement in previous chapters. It could be anything from the computer system failing, a voice message on the telephone system with the wrong opening times, to a failure to put a forwarding email address or alternative contact number for your customers on your out-of-office notification while you are away on holiday.

Performance evidence activity 3

To help with planning your evidence, make notes about some situations where you have experienced:

- a problem that you or your colleague identified before the customer
- a problem you handed over to a colleague.

For both examples, the cause of the problem should be a difference between customer expectations and what is offered by your organisation.

Evidence in context

An example of sample evidence for some of the learning outcomes of Unit C1 has been included at the end of the book.

LEARNER EVALUATION ACTIVITY

The last activity is the learner evaluation. Each section in this chapter is intended to help you to develop yourself towards being a more thinking and reflective customer service professional. The learner evaluation requires you to reflect on your learning from completing this unit guide. Once again, this does not have to be written; however, it could be useful to record your answers for use in reviews with your line manager, supervisor, assessor, tutor or possibly in a job interview.

Documenting your learning throughout your working life is an effective way of showing that you use experience to influence your performance and behaviours. Reflect on what you knew at the start of the unit and what you know now.

1. What have you learned from completing this unit?
2. Identify three phrases that were new to you.
3. How will completing this unit impact on your customer service within your organisation?
4. Highlight an improvement that you have made as a result of completing the unit.

If you are working towards Unit D3 Develop personal performance through delivering customer service, your evaluations might provide you with some foundation evidence.

Summary

This concludes the unit guidance for Unit C1 Recognise and deal with customer queries, requests and problems.

You should be prepared to submit evidence for both the knowledge and performance aspects of the unit learning outcomes:

LO1: Recognise and deal with customer queries and requests
LO2: Recognise and deal with customer problems
LO3: Know how to recognise and deal with customer queries, requests and problems

You will now be able to describe how you recognise and deal with customer requests, queries and problems, interpreting when your customer is dissatisfied or angry. You should be able to evidence how you ask colleagues for help and provide an effective handover if you are unable to deal with a problem.

It is likely that the knowledge and performance evidence you produce for this unit will cross-reference to the following Customer Service units:

- Unit A4 Give customers a positive impression of yourself and your organisation
- Unit A10 Dealing with customers face to face
- Unit D1 Develop customer relationships
- Unit F1 Communicate using customer service language.

DEVELOP CUSTOMER RELATIONSHIPS

Learning outcomes

Learning outcomes for Unit D1:

1. Build their customer's confidence that the service they give will be excellent

2. Meet the expectations of their customers

3. Develop the long-term relationship between their customer and their organisation

4. Know how to develop customer relationships

Introduction

This unit guide is a resource to help you gather the evidence that you require to achieve Unit D1, one of the optional units in the 'Development and improvement' theme of the Level 2 NVQ Certificate in Customer Service. It can be used as a learning resource if you are new to your role, are studying customer service in preparation for work or as a refresher if you are an experienced customer service professional.

Develop customer relationships – what is Unit D1 about?

When you deal with the same customers regularly, you will want to make each occasion a good customer experience. The impression you create and the way the service is delivered affects this in just the same way as when you deal with a customer only once. However, a longer-term relationship with a repeat customer also depends on building up your customer's confidence in the service that you offer. Loyalty and a long-term relationship rely on the customer having a realistic view of the organisation's service and being comfortable with it. Your customer will return to their organisation if they feel confident that they will receive excellent service because they have enjoyed good customer experiences with you before.

Source: Adapted from Unit D1 purpose and aim

To complete this unit you will need to demonstrate how you provide consistent service to all of your customers, particularly those whom you deal with on a regular or repeat basis. Often your regular customers have a higher expectation of the products and services that you and your organisation can offer, so you have to work harder to maintain the relationship, their loyalty and the 'delight' factor. To maintain this level of service you will have to build an honest and open rapport with your customer. This means making them feel valued and, where possible, being able to seek constructive feedback from them. By doing so, you will enable the relationship to flourish.

Completing this unit guide

To complete this unit guide you will need to:

1. Read through the information in each section.

2. Look at the case study and reflective activity and use the questions to help you to test your understanding.

There is no set format for working through or recording your answers in these sections, just use them in a way that suits your learning style, unless otherwise instructed by your assessor or tutor. The case study and reflective activity are linked to the assessment criteria in learning outcome 4, which focuses on the underpinning knowledge and understanding for Unit D1. Learning outcome 4 has been presented first so that you understand the background to the assessment criteria relating to your work performance in learning outcomes 1, 2 and 3. If you work through this section first you will find that your performance evidence will be easier to identify and present to your assessor.

Learning outcome 4 – Knowledge evidence

LO4 Know how to develop customer relationships

● The tutorial section is designed to explain the assessment criteria. In this section your virtual advisor will provide you with information to help you interpret the national standards.

● The case study and reflective activity will help you to prepare to discuss and explain your understanding of customer service with your assessor.

Learning outcomes 1, 2 and 3 – Performance evidence

● **LO1** Build their customer's confidence that the service they give will be excellent

● **LO2** Meet the expectations of their customers

● **LO3** Develop the long-term relationship between their customer and their organisation

In addition to the learning outcomes, in this unit there are performance **evidence requirements** that indicate the circumstances or conditions under which you should present the evidence.

Your communication with customers may be face to face, in writing, by telephone, text message, email, internet (including social networking), intranet or any other method you are expected to use within your job role.

You must provide evidence of taking actions to meet the needs and expectations of your customer and of your organisation:

- without being asked by your customer
- at your customer's request.

You must include evidence that you have balanced the needs of your customers and your organisation by:

- making use of alternative products or services offered by the organisation
- varying the service you would normally offer within organisational guidelines
- saying 'no' to your customer and explaining the limits of your organisation's service offer.

Why do I need to develop my customer relationships?

Customer service is not just a job; it underpins everything you do in your work role. If you are involved in providing products or services to regular customers, whether internal or external to your organisation, it is essential that you are able to:

- behave professionally at all times
- work at the relationship when it is going well and when improvements are required
- build on the relationship by seeking feedback and opinions
- use feedback to find fresh and innovative ways to help your customers.

The cycle of developing excellent customer relationships

The cycle of developing excellent customer relationships illustrates four important stages of a repeat customer service transaction. Regular customers might be internal, such as colleagues from other departments or locations, or external to your organisation.

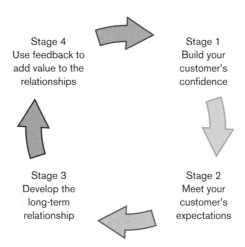

Figure D1.1: The cycle of developing excellent customer relationships

Stage 1 Build your customer's confidence

When dealing with a new or regular customer, it is important to make a good impression by behaving professionally (see Chapter 4 Unit A10) and by creating a rapport with your customer. You can do this by understanding your organisation's expected standards of appearance and behaviour and by empathising with your customer and appreciating their needs. It also involves keeping the promises that you and your organisation make to the customer.

Stage 2 Meet your customer's expectations

Your customer's expectations will influence their relationship with your organisation and therefore you need to be aware of any signals that they are not happy. You looked at dealing with problems and queries in Chapter 7 Unit C1 and the importance of identifying conflict between the customer's expectations and what you can offer. Meeting the expectations of customers, both new and established, involves listening to what they are asking and then seeing whether you can offer an alternative that will suit them. You may have to negotiate with them to reach a happy medium or you may simply have to explain the limits of your service offer.

Stage 3 Develop the long-term relationship

The third stage in the cycle involves developing the long-term relationship between your customer and your organisation. In this process you act as the 'glue', holding together the customer, their needs and expectations, and linking them to the products, services, processes and rules of your organisation. Retaining the loyalty of your customer is vital because there is always another organisation ready to offer something different to them.

Some of the ways that customer service professionals and their organisations 'hook' their customers include loyalty cards, special offers and discounts for long-standing customers. Consistency in the quality of products and services offered are another way of encouraging customers to stay with an organisation.

Stage 4 Use feedback to add value to the relationship

Stage 4 involves asking your customers, both internal and external, for feedback. By inviting your frequent/long-term customers to help your organisation improve its products or services, they become a stakeholder in the business. This can be done through forums, meetings or questionnaires and involves being proactive rather than reacting to historic requests, questions or complaints; you may also be able to provide them with incentives in return for their opinions, ideas and needs. Once this information has been gathered your organisation can look at what its customers really want and add value to the products and services already being offered.

Knowledge evidence for Unit D1 (LO4)

As stated earlier, we will begin with learning outcome 4 (LO4). This contains the knowledge criteria for the unit. In order to sustain and improve in your role as a customer service professional it is essential that you have this knowledge to underpin your performance.

LO4 Know how to develop customer relationships

Assessment criteria

4.1 Describe their organisation's services or products
4.2 Explain the importance of customer retention
4.3 Explain how their own behaviour affects the behaviour of the customer
4.4 Describe how to behave assertively and professionally with customers
4.5 Describe how to defuse potentially stressful situations
4.6 Identify the limitations of their organisation's service offer
4.7 Compare how customer expectations may change as the customer deals with their organisation
4.8 Identify the cost and resource implications of an extension of the service offer to meet or exceed customer expectations
4.9 Explain the cost implications of bringing in new customers as opposed to retaining existing customers
4.10 Identify who to refer to when considering any variation to their organisation's service offer.

TUTORIAL 1 with your virtual advisor:

Read through this tutorial so that you can meet the requirements of the assessment criteria shown above.

4.1 Describe their organisation's services or products

In Chapter 1 Unit F1, Chapter 4 Unit A10 and Chapter 6 Unit B2 we looked at how you can familiarise yourself with your organisation's products and services. This information may be readily available to you through training, meetings and company bulletins, as well as day-to-day tasks like unpacking stock or emails received from suppliers, colleagues and service partners. In addition to this you must be curious and seek additional information so that you are prepared for any questions, information or requests that your customer might make. This might be information on a new version of a product being released in the near future, updated software or changes in service agreements or procedures that might affect the service you provide. The internet or your company intranet is a convenient way to research new developments, product updates, training materials and factual information or simply to see what your competitors are doing. Read trade or professional magazines and journals and talk to experts, developers, managers and trainers so that you get a wider perspective of the sector or market in which you are operating.

You may have already carried out the activity below which linked to assessment criterion 4.1 in Chapter 6 Unit B2. If so, then you can use your answers for this unit too. If not, make some notes so that you can discuss this with your assessor:

Questions

1. Describe three products or services unique to your area of work and identify where you already have, or can obtain, information to extend your knowledge about the products.
2. Talk to a manager or expert in your organisation (or look at the internet or any other sources available) to see if there are any developments, new models or advice that might have an impact on the information your customers will request about the three products or services you identified.

4.2 Explain the importance of customer retention

In Chapter 1 Unit F1 we looked at the use of customer service language. The phrase 'customer retention' simply means keeping or holding your customers! Without your customers you have no business, so it is important that once you have 'hooked' your customers, you keep them.

Questions

Consider the following in relation to your organisation:

1. Who are your regular customers and are they internal or external?
2. What incentives do you use to keep your customers?
3. What do your competitors or other departments do to retain their customer's loyalty?
4. What are the benefits to you and your organisation of keeping your customers?
5. What would happen if you lost your long standing/regular customers?
6. Name four incentives that you have been offered by organisations (as a customer) to keep your loyalty.

Figure D1.2

4.3 Explain how their own behaviour affects the behaviour of the customer

In Chapter 3 Unit A4 you looked at how to establish rapport with your customers and adapt your behaviour to respond to different customer behaviours. First impressions count with a customer and they can make or break an organisation's reputation. You might be the only person that the customer has contact with, so how you look, sound and behave will have an impact on their perception of the organisation.

In Chapter 7 Unit C1 we looked at what is meant by professional behaviour and how your behaviour could make a situation worse. Professional behaviour is vital in any organisation, even if there is a relaxed or casual approach to customer service. Standards of behaviour and language will vary depending on the customer base; what is deemed acceptable with internal customers might have to be adjusted when dealing with external customers. Professional behaviour in any business context needs to be kept in line with legal obligations and decency. It is unacceptable for employees to swear or to treat others in an offensive manner, whether face to face, verbally or in writing.

Questions

1. How are you expected to behave towards your customers?

2. What would happen if you mirrored a customer's anger or sarcasm during a transaction?

3. Think of an example when you have witnessed someone acting unprofessionally during a customer transaction. What were your feelings about the situation? How did it impact on the customer relationship? (You do not need to have been the customer.)

4.4 Describe how to behave assertively and professionally with customers

In Chapter 4 Unit A10 you looked at positive and negative behaviour and, in particular, at the difference between assertive and aggressive behaviour. Assertiveness was defined as confidently putting your point of view over to another without threatening their rights or ignoring or excluding their opinion. It is a strong behaviour but should be non-threatening to the customer.

Assertiveness should always be combined with professional behaviour and can be conveyed through positive body language: good posture, frequent eye contact and smiling (but not grinning or appearing over confident).

Question

1. Describe two customer transactions where you behaved assertively and professionally with your customers. (If you have a statement or feedback from the customer or your manager/colleague you can use this to support your answer.)

4.5 Describe how to defuse potentially stressful situations

There will be times when you identify a potentially stressful situation from the customer's behaviour or language, or from the demands that they are making.

When this happens you will need to listen to the customer and let them have their say without interruption. During the conversation you should be processing what they are saying and linking it to all possible options. Perhaps they are asking for a discount or an exception to the service that you provide, in which case you need to decide if this is something that you can deal with or if you will need to involve your supervisor. In the meantime your facial expressions, spoken language as well as body language will be vital to maintain rapport with your customer. This means:

- smiling (even if you are on the telephone)
- an interested expression (do not appear distracted)
- displaying good posture
- using a calm friendly voice
- using assertive not aggressive behaviour.

Once the customer has finished speaking be sure not to make any promises that you cannot keep.

Questions

1. Describe a potentially stressful situation that you have had with a customer, or one that you have witnessed.
2. How was the situation handled and what action was (or should have been) taken to stop it from becoming a negative experience for the customer?

4.6 Identify the limitations of their organisation's service offer

4.8 Identify the cost and resource implications of an extension of the service offer to meet or exceed customer expectations

4.10 Identify who to refer to when considering any variation to their organisation's service offer

We have looked at the service offer in previous chapters and defined this as a set of standards, a promise, an agreement or an arrangement stating what you can offer to your customer. Sometimes the promise will be worded to comply with statutory obligations relating to data protection or consumer protection laws. In Chapter 7 Unit C1 we also looked at the limits of what you are allowed to do for your customers. The service offer should provide clear guidelines so that you are fair and equitable to all of your customers.

An example of a service offer could be a requirement to return a customer's telephone call or respond to their email within 24 hours. This might arise because on average there are 100 messages to respond to each day and it may be reasonable for only 25 messages to be dealt with by one person. Therefore, if there are five people in your department it is feasible to get back to the customer within 24 hours; this also makes allowances for team member absence. If a customer then asks you to get back to them within two hours, under the terms of the service offer this could be seen as an unreasonable or impossible request. When dealing with such a customer you will need to explain clearly and give your reasons why the service offer cannot be met. Show the customer in what you say and/or your actions that you want to do everything possible to meet their needs but explain the limitations of the service offer. It might be possible to offer a compromise and offer to get back to them in five hours. You will need to know what is possible and what cannot be achieved by having a thorough understanding of your organisation's policies and procedures and discussions with your manager and colleagues.

Your organisation might have a policy of allowing customers to return goods within 28 days from purchase; however, there might be exceptions to this if goods are faulty or not fit for the purpose the customer bought them for. Once again, it is vital that you understand why the service offer is made and the impact on costs if the customer requests an extension to it. It is important that you identify who can make decisions that are outside the limits of your authority. When you are looking at a solution to satisfy your customer's needs you also have to be realistic about what you can do for them. It would not be a sound decision to promise to get back to a customer within five hours if you know that there is no one available to deal with the customer for at least six hours. Any decision made must also be based on the costs to the organisation; this could be in terms of money, time, people or even legal requirements. Do not be afraid to ask a colleague or supervisor to give a second opinion if the customer does not seem to be confident in your decision.

Questions

1. Identify the limitations of your organisation's service offer/agreements/promises.

2. Give an example of a request that you could not fulfil because it was outside the limits of the service offer or agreement.

3. How does your organisation extend the service offer to its customers? Provide two examples of when this has happened.

4. Who do you need to consult if you make an extension to the service offer?

5. What costs and resources do you need to think about if and when you extend the service offer for the customer?

4.7 Compare how customer expectations may change as the customer deals with their organisation

When a customer is new to an organisation they have a limited understanding of the products or services they are able to access and the procedures that drive the delivery of customer service. However, if they become a regular user they will become familiar with what the organisation can offer. Over time their expectations may change. Here are the stages in an example of a customer buying a new car from a car dealership.

Stage 1: Purchase period – information gathering and purchase of the car.

Stage 2: Warranty period – milestone checks, servicing and repairs to minor problems.

Stage 3: Trade in period – sale of the old car and purchase of a new car when warranty has expired.

During the three-year period and at each stage, the customer's expectations will change. After the purchase they will know more about the brand and their immediate needs of wanting a car will have been satisfied. They will now have a new set of needs – the security of having regular service checks and minor faults addressed. The organisation has to retain the customer's goodwill to the brand and the organisation so they need to involve them in the feedback process after every customer contact (at purchase, servicing and any other time they bring the car into the dealership) to ensure that they understand the customer's expectations and develop and retain their loyalty to the brand. Ultimately the dealer wants the customer to buy a new car with them again and therefore gain repeat business. The aim of any organisation is to exceed customer expectations within budget and to delight their customers with the service provided.

Questions

1. How do your customers' expectations change during their relationship with your organisation?

2. Think about your products or services. How do you promote them to your established customers?

3. What repeat business do you get from your customers and why?

4.9 Explain the cost implications of bringing in new customers as opposed to retaining existing customers

It is a well known fact that retaining a customer will cost your business far less than finding new customers. Satisfied customers are very helpful to an organisation as they spread the news of good customer service; this is free marketing for an organisation. Overall it is easier to do business with existing customers than with customers new to your organisation. When you look for new customers you have to research, promote and invest resources in attracting people who have no loyalty to your brand and who may already be happy with the service from a competitor. Even if they are not completely satisfied with your competitors, most customers do not want to change unless they really have to.

Building a customer base is a lengthy process and investment in this might, in the end, fail to bring in the result that you wanted. If you have a good customer base already then it is important to use this information. Find out who your customers are, build an accurate database of facts and figures about their use of your services and their likes, needs and must haves. For example, in some hotels, staff are expected to find out at least five preferences that each and every customer has. This information helps the staff to assess the customer's likes, needs and must haves and to delight them by providing a quick response. Take time to ask your customers questions and involve them in testing, sampling and evaluating your products and services. Many organisations within the retail sector, particularly supermarkets and mobile phone companies, are aggressive in building their existing customers' history on a database.

Questions

1. List some of the methods that retailers have of building on their existing customer base.

2. Talk to your manager, supervisor or colleagues and discuss how your organisation attracts new customers and how much this costs. Compare this with how much it costs to promote your goods and services to existing customers.

3. How do you find out what your existing customers want, need and must have?

The case study below provides an opportunity for you to read about a customer service professional and consolidates some of the information from the tutorial. You can use this to reflect on the situation and answer some questions. You do not have to write your answers down unless your tutor or assessor has asked you to do so.

CASE STUDY 1

Hannah works for an insurance company handling policies for a major supermarket in the UK. Today she received a telephone call from a customer who had received some information in the post about a special offer of a free camera if she was to take out a new policy for pet insurance. The customer already had two cats insured with the organisation and had just received a renewal for the next year in the post. The price was considerably higher than her annual policy last year and Hannah could hear from the customer's tone of voice that she was concerned and a little dissatisfied with this.

The customer wanted to know how she could claim her free gift and whether she was entitled to it as she was an existing customer. Hannah was able to bring the customer's details up on her screen and could see the full history of the customer's purchasing of policies and claims over the last three years. She could see that the customer had been loyal to the organisation. Hannah went through the details of the policy and asked the customer for details about her cats. Hannah checked the details against her records and could see the price quoted for the new policy was in excess of what it would cost if she set up a brand new policy for the customer. She asked the customer for all the details about her cats and then she calculated the policy price.

Hannah made a quick decision to advise the customer that if she took out a new policy for her cats she would not only be entitled to the free gift, she would also have a reduction in the cost of her annual policy. She knew that she was allowed to do this, particularly if a customer challenged the difference between the phone quote and the written quote, as this had been covered in staff training recently. The customer was delighted as the new quote was at least £3 a month cheaper than the postal quote.

Hannah also explained to the customer that she had received a discount because she held the supermarket loyalty card. Hannah went on to explain the legal requirements of taking out an insurance policy. After each section she checked the customer's understanding. Hannah then had an opportunity to add value to the customer's policy and quoted additional cover for a slightly higher annual cost. This price still came below the customer's original postal quote. She allowed her customer time to think about this extension to the service offer. The customer then decided to take the additional cover.

Hannah concluded the transaction by explaining how the customer could claim her special offer and the legal protection that the customer was entitled to. The customer expressed her delight with Hannah's helpfulness and product knowledge. Hannah then took the opportunity to ask the customer if she minded answering a few questions about her lifestyle and her cats and the preferences that they had for food and where she purchased it from. Once she had finished with the customer Hannah recorded the information on the database and updated the customer's history.

Questions

1. What extensions to the service offer did Hannah highlight to her customer?

2. What did the organisation offer to the customer for loyalty?

3. How did Hannah build up a history of this customer during this transaction?

4. How did Hannah find out what she was allowed to offer to her customer?

The reflective activity below is designed to help you to start thinking about the concept of the service offer and customer loyalty and how this can be developed. We are all customers on a regular basis, so the first question in the activity is from the perspective of you as the customer; the remaining questions are from the perspective of you as a customer service professional. It will help to prepare you to collect evidence that will demonstrate your knowledge, understanding and practical skills in customer service. Write down your reflections if you wish as they may be useful in discussions or questioning sessions with your assessor or in the preparation of evidence.

REFLECTIVE ACTIVITY

1. Think of an organisation you use on a regular basis. What have you been offered by the organisation to try to retain your loyalty? How effective was the incentive?
2. List three ways that you could improve customer retention and loyalty in your branch/ department/organisation.
3. What are the costs and what resources will you need to improve customer retention?
4. Who will you need to discuss your ideas with?

Performance evidence for Unit D1 (LO1, LO2 and LO3)

The case study and reflective activity have given you the opportunity to consider the customer service provided in different customer service settings and to think about the customer experience.

The next section in this unit is designed to help you focus on the learning outcomes and performance requirement of Unit D1 and prompt you to think how you can evidence this through your customer service role. It is expected that the evidence that you generate for this unit will also cross-reference with some of the optional units that you have selected. Your virtual advisor will guide you to collect the evidence that you need to complete this unit.

LO1 Build their customer's confidence that the service they give will be excellent

Assessment criteria
1.1 Show that they behave assertively and professionally with customers
1.2 Allocate the time they take to deal with their customer following organisational guidelines
1.3 Reassure their customer that they are doing everything possible to keep the service promises made by the organisation

In learning outcome 4 we examined the knowledge criteria that will demonstrate that you have an understanding of your organisation's products and services and how to develop customer relationships with established or regular customers, including how you behave towards them. You should be able to explain the importance of this behaviour and knowledge to your assessor.

To meet the requirements of assessment criterion 1.1 you need to ensure that every time you deal with a customer your behaviour is positive and professional. We have looked at how to behave professionally in Chapter 7 Unit C1 (assessment criteria 3.3) and how to create a rapport with customers in Chapter 4 Unit A10. When dealing with customers you need to be sure you conform to your organisation's expectations and those of your customer. This includes the messages you send out to your customer in the way you dress, the verbal language you use and the body language that you convey. However, it is not just the messages that you give out that are important; the messages your customer provides to you, and how you interpret them, are equally important and require you to use careful, active and empathetic listening and to look for signals and clues from your customer of their satisfaction or otherwise. Sometimes you will be required to use assertive behaviour in order to take control of a situation and you can do so by acting in a firm but polite manner.

Assessment criterion 1.2 requires you to allocate your time appropriately when dealing with customers and in line with your organisation's guidelines. Think about the standards of service or service offer set by your organisation and how you maintain these. For example, you might be expected to answer the phone within three rings or communicate with your customer within 24 hours. You will also have other internal standards set by your organisation. This might involve completing a report by the end of each calendar month for an internal customer.

Adhering to standards will affect the time you can allocate to your customers and it is vital that you plan your time around the guidelines set by your organisation. There are many ways in which you can do this:

- Keep a daily 'to do' list or a team handover book so that others can see what has been achieved and what still needs to be done.
- Use the calendar software on your computer and set reminders.
- Use post-it notes displayed in a prominent place.
- Put message reminders on your telephone
- Keep a log of activities that you have undertaken during the day (your supervisor may require you to do this).

Whatever method you choose, it is important to prioritise and complete the actions and activities so that you meet both organisation and customer expectations. Use your systems to evidence this part of the qualification.

Figure D1.3

Assessment criterion 1.3 is about explaining and reassuring your customer that you are doing whatever you can to keep the service promises made by your organisation. Look back at the case study in Chapter 7 Unit C1. Ivor was a regular customer who did not experience service that matched the organisation's service promises in terms of response to requested feedback. After mentioning this to a number of customer service professionals at Windruffs and B&S Insurance he did at last receive reassurance that his feedback was being looked at. However, by the end of the case study Ivor had still not received an explanation about what happened or an apology. In terms of time and resources it would have been more cost effective for B&S Insurance to have reacted to Ivor's first incidence of feedback made by telephone. Having to investigate the incident several months later will involve more time and effort by the B&S Insurance supervisor who has now been asked to look into the case.

Performance evidence activity 1

Look again at the examples you produced for assessment criteria 4.4 earlier in this chapter and use them as a basis for your evidence to meet the requirements of learning outcome 1. You can also evidence learning outcome 1 through observation by your assessor or through witness statements from your manager. Prepare some notes to help you plan the sources of your evidence. In addition:

1. List the names of your regular or long-term customers.

2. What resources do you use to allocate your time to deal with customers in line with your organisation's guidelines?

3. Provide an example of how you have reassured a customer that you are doing everything possible to keep your service promise and provide an excellent service. How did you know that you had been successful?

LO2 Meet the expectations of their customers

> ### Assessment criteria
> 2.1 Recognise when there may be a conflict between their customer's expectations and your organisation's service offer
> 2.2 Balance their customer's expectations with their organisation's service offer by offering an alternative or explaining the limits of the service offer
> 2.3 Work effectively with others to resolve any difficulties in meeting their customer's expectations

TUTORIAL 3 with your virtual advisor:

In learning outcome 4 we looked at how to diffuse potentially stressful situations and identify the limitations of your organisation's service offer. There will be times when you have realised through your customer's reactions and language that what you are able to offer to them is less than they expected. This could be in terms of price – maybe this is different to the advertised price. It could also be in terms of delivery times or when a customer fails to see the small print in the terms and conditions.

It is important that you identify such conflict and react to it. It could be that you are able to offer an alternative that meets the customer's needs, even though it was not what they originally requested. Sometimes however you will have to explain that you cannot do anything. When explaining to the customer you need to be as honest and open as possible. Do not appear to blame others as this will appear unprofessional. Instead, let your customer know the processes or reasoning behind the decision.

Remember you can only offer a customer an alternative solution if you have the processes and procedures to support it within the organisation and it will not have major cost implications. In some circumstances an organisation will be able to offer a goodwill gesture such as a voucher, a one-off free product or service or a refund if the impact on customer satisfaction will result in disproportionate dissatisfaction. If you cannot make the decision on your own you need to explain this to the customer and seek the assistance of a colleague who can decide the outcome.

Performance evidence activity 2

For learning outcome 2 identify and describe:

1. A situation when you recognised that your customer's expectations were more than you were able to offer and you had to tell them why you could not help. Provide details of how you did this.

2. A situation where the customer identified that they were not happy with the service offer but you were able to offer an alternative product or service.

3. A situation where you varied the service (within organisational guidelines) that you would normally offer. This could be where you made the decision on your own or you had to consult with a manager or colleague to do this. Explain what you had to consider when you varied the service.

LO3 Develop the long-term relationship between their customer and their organisation

Assessment criteria

3.1 Give additional help and information to their customer in response to customer questions and comments about their organisation's services or products

3.2 Discuss expectations with their customer and explain how these compare with their organisation's services or products

3.3 Advise others of feedback received from their customer

3.4 Identify new ways of helping customers based on the feedback customers have given them

3.5 Identify added value that their organisation could offer to long-term customers

TUTORIAL 4 with your virtual advisor:

Criterion 3.1 is best evidenced through observation or discussion with your assessor. However, you should also make notes about some customer transactions where you have provided additional help and information in response to customer questions and comments. (You might have provided some examples of this already for learning outcome 2 of this unit or from the activities in Chapter 7 Unit C1. Your assessor will be able to advise you about maximising observation and discussion opportunities and wherever possible you should cross-reference evidence from other units in the qualification. Support your statements and discussions with emails, letters, customer database information or statements from your manager, colleagues or even customers. This time it is important for you to record your answers in writing, as this will be the foundation of your evidence, but you need only make notes to prompt you where the proof is located.

To meet the requirements of assessment criteria 3.2–3.4 you must be sure to take notice of all comments that your customers make about the products or services that you and your organisation provide. Feedback might be formally requested through a follow-up telephone call, questionnaire or customer forum. However, the most valuable feedback often comes from verbal comments and it is a good idea to write these down when you receive them. You might have a system or procedure to record the comments on a customer file or if there is no formal procedure then a notebook, accessible to your manager and colleagues, can be an effective alternative. Always share formal and informal feedback with others in the organisation or your service partners. It might come in useful when you are justifying an improvement or discussing service levels with your colleagues. This information will also shape the future of the products or services that you offer because it is an indication of your customers' needs and expectations.

Figure D1.4: Capture feedback at every opportunity

Assessment criterion 3.5 refers to 'added value' but what is added value? This is defined as any extra offer, over and above the basic product or normal service offer that you make to your customers. For example, additional information on a report, or if a long-term customer has spent a large amount of money with the organisation something as simple as a branded, fabric carrier bag for their purchase, a bouquet of flowers in their new car or an offer of a soft toy if they use a new product or service. This added value will have a small cost implication but the delight factor will often outweigh the cost.

Performance evidence activity 3

Give two examples of how you have collected feedback from your customer, one formal and one informal:

1. How did you record this feedback?
2. What did this feedback tell you?
3. What new ways of helping customers have you implemented as a result of this feedback?
4. Identify two opportunities to offer added value to your long-term customers.

TUTORIAL 4 with your virtual advisor:

Evidence requirements provide the context in which you meet the assessment criteria for performance and enable your assessor to judge whether you are competent in a number of different situations. You do not need to cover the evidence requirements separately; they will be covered as you complete the assessment criteria. Your assessor will give you guidance. The evidence requirements for Unit D1 are explained below:

● *Your communication with customers may be face to face, in writing, by telephone, text message, email, internet (including social networking), intranet or by any other method you would be expected to use within your job role.*

● *You must provide evidence of taking actions to meet the needs and expectations of your customer and of your organisation without being asked by your customer.*

● *You must provide evidence of taking actions to meet the needs and expectations of your customer and of your organisation at your customer's request.*

The evidence requirements shown above should have been embedded into some of the examples that you have already identified in the activities in this chapter. If you have not provided an example for both evidence requirements discuss this with your assessor.

● *You must include evidence that you have balanced the needs of your customers and your organisation by:*

   – *making use of alternative products or services offered by the organisation*

   – *varying the service you would normally offer within organisational guidelines*

   – *saying 'no' to your customer and explaining the limits of your organisation's service offer.*

Make sure that the examples that you have already given in performance evidence activity 2 contain the three requirements of balancing the needs of your customer and your organisation. You might find the answers you gave to the questions following assessment criterion 4.4 will be helpful here as well.

The last activity is the learner evaluation. Each section in this chapter is intended to help you to develop yourself towards being a more thinking and reflective customer service professional. The learner evaluation requires you to reflect on your learning from completing this unit guide. Once again, this does not have to be written; however, it could be useful to record your answers for use in reviews with your line manager, supervisor, assessor, tutor or possibly in a job interview.

Documenting your learning throughout your working life is a very effective way of showing that you use experience to influence your performance and behaviours. Reflect on what you knew at the start of the unit and what you know now.

1. What have you learned from completing this unit?

2. Identify three phrases that were new to you.

3. How will completing this unit impact on your customer service within your organisation?

4. Highlight an improvement that you have made as a result of completing the unit.

If you are working towards Unit D3 Develop personal performance through delivering customer service, your evaluations might provide you with some foundation evidence.

Summary

This concludes the unit guidance for Unit D1 Develop customer relationships.

You should be prepared to submit evidence for both the knowledge and performance aspects of the unit learning outcomes:

LO1: Build their customer's confidence that the service they give will be excellent

LO2: Meet the expectations of their customers

LO3: Develop the long-term relationship between their customer and their organisation

LO4: Know how to develop customer relationships

You will now be able to describe how you value and develop your customer relationships, balancing the needs of the customer and the organisation and doing everything possible to keep your organisation's service promises and offers.

It is likely that the knowledge and performance evidence you produce for this unit will cross-reference to the following Customer Service units:

- Unit A4 Give your customer a positive impression of yourself and your organisation

- Unit A10 Deal with customers face to face

- Unit B2 Deliver reliable customer service

- Unit C1 Recognise and deal with customer queries requests and problems

- Unit F1 Communicate using customer service language.

DEVELOP PERSONAL PERFORMANCE THROUGH DELIVERING CUSTOMER SERVICE

Learning outcomes

> **Learning outcomes for Unit D3:**
> **1.** Review performance in their customer service role
> **2.** Prepare a personal development plan and keep it up to date
> **3.** Undertake development activities and obtain feedback on their customer service performance
> **4.** Understand how to develop their personal performance through delivering customer service

This unit guide is a resource to help you gather the evidence that you require to achieve Unit D3, one of the optional units in the 'Development and improvement' theme of the Level 2 NVQ Certificate in Customer Service. It can be used as a learning resource if you are new to your role, are studying customer service in preparation for work or as a refresher if you are an experienced customer service professional.

Develop personal performance through delivering customer service – what is Unit D3 about?

Delivering customer service presents many opportunities for learning and for developing personal skills. This unit is about how you can develop your personal skills at the same time as improving your customer service performance. You will need to plan together with a manager or mentor and then carry out activities which help you learn and develop in your customer service role. Customer service improvements rely on continuous improvement and this includes improving your own skills.

Source: Adapted from Unit D3 purpose and aim

To complete the unit you will need to demonstrate your understanding of how to identify your strengths and your areas for improvement as a customer service professional. You need to reflect on and review your performance with an appropriate person, for example, your manager, supervisor, team leader, mentor or a learning and development expert. You are required to set up a development plan to help you learn and develop your skills, knowledge and understanding in your customer service role. Finally, you will need to demonstrate how you carry the development activities through to a conclusion.

Completing this unit guide

To complete this unit guide you will need to:

1. Read through the information in each section.

2. Look at the case study and reflective activity and use the questions to help you to test your understanding.

There is no set format for working through or recording your answers in these sections, just use them in a way that suits your learning style, unless otherwise instructed by your assessor or tutor. The case study and reflective activity are linked to the assessment criteria in learning outcome 4, which focuses on the underpinning knowledge and understanding for unit D3. Learning outcome 4 has been presented first so that you understand the background to the criteria in learning outcomes 1, 2 and 3. If you work through this section first you will find that your performance evidence will be easier to identify and present to your assessor.

The reflective customer service professional

Learning is something we do all the time but we are often unaware that it is happening. As a baby we learned how to walk, talk and get on with other children and adults. This was done unconsciously and the only people to reflect on our learning were the people who cared for us in our early years. Many of us will have baby books where the key milestones in our development were painstakingly and proudly recorded.

Students in schools and colleges are now encouraged to evaluate and reflect on activities that they have undertaken in order to harvest their learning; this is part of the lifelong learning journey. Often we only consider learning to have taken place on structured courses and through reading books; we may overlook the learning we gain from day-to-day events. Learning is not something that is done to you; you are at the heart of the learning process and as a customer service professional it is your responsibility to reflect on your practices, take responsibility for your learning and do something useful with it.

There are many models of learning styles and one of the most famous was published by David Kolb in 1984. This is a well-documented theory of learning represented by an experiential learning cycle. Many learning tools, such as learning styles questionnaires, have evolved from Kolb's model and are frequently used in schools, colleges and the workplace. You may have completed a Honey and Mumford's learning styles questionnaire (see Tutorial 1), either in the past or more recently when you started this qualification. Correctly applied, this questionnaire can help you to understand how you learn and what methods of learning you enjoy or prefer the most. Another type of learning style identification is the VAK theory:

- **V**isual – learning through seeing and reading
- **A**udio – learning through listening and speaking
- **K**inesthetic – learning through touching and doing.

Your VAK learning style can also be identified by completing a questionnaire and follow-up guidance. There is a wealth of information about different learning styles and their accompanying questionnaires available on the internet (try for example www.businessballs.com, then click on the link to multiple intelligences and VAK) as well as many reference books.

Learning outcome 4 – Knowledge evidence

LO4 Understand how to develop their personal performance through delivering customer service

- The tutorial section is designed to explain the assessment criteria. In this section your virtual advisor will provide you with information to help you interpret the national standards.

- The case study and reflective activity will help you to prepare to discuss and explain your understanding of how you can develop your personal performance through delivering customer service with your assessor.

Learning outcomes 1, 2 and 3 – Performance evidence

LO1 Review performance in their customer service role (with an appropriate person)
LO2 Prepare a personal development plan and keep it up to date
LO3 Undertake development activities and obtain feedback on their customer service performance

In addition to the learning outcomes, in this unit there are performance evidence requirements that indicate the circumstances or conditions under which you should present the evidence. You are required to review your performance and present your evidence to an appropriate person.

An 'appropriate person' must be one or more of the following:

- your manager
- your supervisor or team leader
- a colleague detailed to help you learn
- your assessor
- your mentor
- someone from your training or personnel department.

You must provide evidence that you have developed your personal development plan, taking account of:

- information about the knowledge and skills relevant to your customer service role
- your own learning style preferences
- your workload
- opportunities for learning on the job.

Your personal development plan must be put on record and agreed with an appropriate person.

The customer service professional's learning cycle

The learning cycle (see Figure D3.1) is based on planning, doing, reviewing and concluding (drawing out learning points).

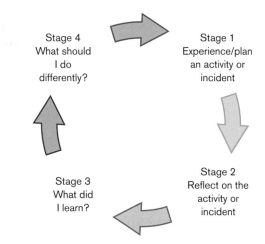

Stage 4
What should
I do
differently?

Stage 1
Experience/plan
an activity or
incident

Stage 3
What did
I learn?

Stage 2
Reflect on the
activity or
incident

Figure D3.1: The customer service professional's learning cycle

Stage 1 Experience/plan an activity or incident

Whether as a customer service professional or a customer, you will be experiencing incidents and/or planning activities as part of your day-to-day work, while on a training course, when speaking to colleagues and experts or through research.

Stage 2 Reflect on the activity or incident

It is important to reflect on each activity or incident by asking yourself what happened and why did it happen.

Stage 3 What did I learn?

Take time to think about the learning points from the incident or activity. What have you gained through the experience? Making notes so that you know what to do next time you encounter a similar situation may be helpful. You might already be discussing these events with your assessor when you are planning your evidence for this qualification, or your assessor or supervisor might have observed you in action and provided you with feedback on how to improve your skills or knowledge. Use these opportunities to discuss what you have gained from the events or the feedback.

Stage 4 What should I do differently?

The final stage involves evaluating what has happened, what you have learned and whether the next time you encounter the same or a similar situation you would do things differently. This is the stage that really demonstrates that you are a reflective customer service professional and that you have embedded the learning that has taken place to consolidate new learning, build on a positive experience or avoid a repeat of a negative event.

By going through the four stages each time a new or significant incident or activity arises you will consciously reflect and learn in a positive and structured way. You have been asked to reflect in each chapter of the book within the reflective activity. If you apply the learning cycle when you carry out this reflection activity you will be able to add to your customer service skills, knowledge and understanding.

Knowledge evidence for Unit D3 (LO4)

As stated earlier, we are starting with learning outcome 4 (LO4). This contains the knowledge criteria for the unit. In order to sustain and improve in your role as a customer service professional it is essential that you have this knowledge to underpin your performance.

LO4 Understand how to develop their personal performance through delivering customer service

Assessment criteria
4.1 Describe their organisation's systems and procedures for developing personal performance in customer service
4.2 Explain how their behaviour has an effect on the behaviour of others
4.3 Explain how effective learning depends on a process of planning, doing and reviewing
4.4 Describe how to review effectively their personal strengths and development needs
4.5 Describe how to put together a personal development plan that will build on their strengths and overcome their weaknesses in areas that are important to customer service
4.6 Explain how to access sources of information and support for their learning
4.7 Explain how to obtain useful and constructive personal feedback from others
4.8 Describe how to respond positively to personal feedback

TUTORIAL 1 with your virtual advisor:

Read through this tutorial so that you can meet the requirements of the assessment criteria shown above.

4.1 Describe their organisation's systems and procedures for developing personal performance in customer service

While it is your responsibility to identify what you know and need to learn in your job role, it is also the responsibility of your manager, team leader, supervisor or experts in learning and development within your organisation to support you (these are the 'appropriate people' as mentioned earlier in this chapter).

When you are new to your role you are not expected to know everything; usually you will be given an induction or training period to help you settle into the new job and to ensure that you know and understand the rules, regulations and laws that affect your customer service provision (see Chapter 2 Unit F2). It is important that your training and learning is documented to prove that you have been given the necessary information, particularly in the case of health and safety, data protection and equality regulations as well as any other legislation that could impact on your ability to provide customer service. If this has not happened then ask the appropriate person if there is proof of your training on record.

Once you are fully competent in the basic requirements of your job there should be a process of reviewing your customer service performance with the appropriate person. This should be a two-way process that will provide an opportunity for you to discuss and identify what you need to do to develop yourself. There should be processes and documents in place within your organisation to help you to access learning and development opportunities and discuss them with the appropriate person. If you cannot find any information in your organisation, use the documents included in this chapter.

Below are some documents that can help you record and reflect on your customer service learning.

- Learning log: use this to record a list of experiential learning activities, the date the activity took place and comments to remind you what you gained from the activity (Figure D3.2).

- A reflective record: use this to record details of an incident so that you can learn from the experience (Figure D3.3) – see later in this chapter.

Learning log

Date	Learning incident/activity	Comments about the incident/activity

Figure D3.2: Learning log

Reflective record

A Reflective Record for Name: Date:

What happened?	Why did it happen?	What did I learn?	How will I use this learning in the future?

Figure D3.3: Reflective record

4.2 Explain how their behaviour has an effect on the behaviour of others

In Tutorial 1 in Chapter 3 Unit A4, you were asked to describe your organisation's standards for personal appearance and behaviour; understanding the standards that are acceptable within your organisation is important. The 'others' referred to in the assessment criterion might be colleagues carrying out the same or a similar role to you, internal customers, service partners (see Chapter 2 Unit F2, Tutorial 1), managers or learning and development experts within your organisation. Your behaviour, verbal and body language and written communications will affect your area of work and the impression you give to others. Behaviour in any business context needs to be kept in line with legal obligations and decency. In Chapter 8 Unit D1, Tutorial 1, you looked at building rapport with your customers, especially over a period of time. The same rules apply to building relationships with others in your organisation.

Sometimes when you receive feedback you might not agree with all that is said or written. In this instance it is important to demonstrate assertiveness, but not aggressiveness. Assertiveness is defined as confidently putting a point of view over to another without threatening their rights or ignoring or excluding their opinion. It is a strong behaviour but should be non-threatening to the person providing you with the feedback. Assertiveness should always be combined with professional behaviour and can be portrayed through positive body language. We will discuss how to deal with constructive, critical feedback later in the chapter.

Questions

1. Describe the standards of behaviour in place in your organisation.

2. Explain how your behaviour could affect others in your area of work that provide you with support, guidance or feedback.

4.3 Explain how effective learning depends on a process of planning, doing and reviewing

Look back again at the stages of the learning cycle at the beginning of this chapter to see how effective learning involves planning, doing and reviewing. Every time you experience a significant incident, learn about a new product or service or carry out any learning activity, you need to think about how this has affected you and how it has improved your customer service. Resources have been included in this chapter to help you carry out this planning, doing and reviewing.

4.4 Describe how to review effectively their personal strengths and development needs

A customer service SWOT (strengths, weaknesses, opportunities and threats) analysis will help you to examine your current situation in regard to your personal strengths and help you to identify areas for development.

- Strengths – focus on what you are good at, for example, your specialist knowledge of products and processes, dealing with certain types of customers, your communication skills.

- Opportunities – identify where an offer of help would develop your skills, knowledge and understanding. Sometimes we have to invest time (without monetary reward) to produce benefits at a later date. For example, a new product range is coming in so to help train colleagues, offer to research it, talk to experts and find out what your competitors are offering. If a new member of staff is joining your department, offer to be their buddy or mentor. Being willing to take on extra responsibility will often help with your own development.

- Weaknesses or areas for improvement – use the reflective approach (the experiential learning cycle and reflective activities in this book) to honestly analyse where you could improve your skills, knowledge and understanding. You can also use customer and colleague feedback (e.g. mystery shopper exercises, questionnaires, informal comments, one to one meetings) to help you identify where you can improve.

- Threats – the threats to your learning are going to be particular to you and your workplace. For example, you might be a part-time worker and this will affect your opportunity to join in team meetings or training events. The business might be suffering from staff shortages or lack of finance and this might impact on learning opportunities. You might not have a development review with your manager.

An example of a completed SWOT analysis is shown below (Figure D3.4).

4.5 Describe how to put together a personal development plan that will build on their strengths and overcome their weaknesses in areas that are important to customer service

When you identify what you need to do to improve your personal customer service performance you must document this so that you and your appropriate person know that you have a target or goal to achieve. Such a document is often referred to as a development plan and should be linked to your personal performance objectives (these are often recorded in a performance review).

Your personal objectives might link with the customer promise, service level agreement, mission or standards that your organisation sets for each customer service professional, or they might emerge from your SWOT or reflective activities. If you do not have a document in place to identify your performance objectives or record your development activities you might find the development plan shown below useful (Figure D3.5). A development plan for your customer service role usually requires you to ask yourself:

- What do I want/need to do/learn?
- What will I do to achieve it?
- What resources/support will I need?
- How will I know I have achieved this learning?
- Target date for review and completion.

SWOT ANALYSIS

Strengths
Focus on your positive customer service qualities

List what you can do and have done

What specialist knowledge do you have?
What are the strong parts of your character?
What qualities and skills do you have?
What is the strength of your professional reputation?
What has helped you succeed in your job?

HOW WILL YOU OPTIMISE YOUR STRENGTHS?

Weaknesses
Take into account the weaknesses that you can deal with.

Focus on those aspects of yourself and your current customer service role that you wish to improve.
When dealing with customers:
What are the weak points of your customer service skills?
What gaps are there in your knowledge and understanding?
What are the weak points when reacting to difficult situations?
In what areas could you improve your communication skills?

HOW WILL YOU TURN THE WEAKNESSES INTO STRENGTHS?

Opportunities
What do you want to achieve both professionally and personally in the future?

Be realistic!

What do you want to achieve over the next year?
What goals do you want to fulfil in the next 3–5 years?
What is currently happening that is a positive force in your job and life?
What are the opportunities that will allow you to develop?

HOW WILL YOU MAXIMISE THE OPPORTUNITIES?

Threats
What might stop you achieving your opportunities and goals?

Be practical!

What are the changes/influences that might affect your current situation?
What might hinder you and your learning and development?
What people or processes might get in the way?

HOW WILL YOU OVERCOME THESE THREATS?

Figure D3.4: SWOT analysis

DEVELOPMENT PLAN

A Development Plan for   Name: Date:

What do I want/need to do/learn?	What will I do to achieve this?	What resources/support will I need	How will I know I have achieved this learning?	Target dates for review and completion

Figure D3.5: Development plan

Finally, to complete the learning cycle you should document your thoughts in a reflective record – you will be asked to do this later in the chapter.

Figure D3.6

Question

Make a list or prepare some notes in answer to the questions below for use in discussion with your assessor.

1. What systems and procedures are in place in your organisation to help you to identify your performance objectives?

2. What systems and procedures are in place in your organisation to help you identify your strengths and areas for improvement and record your learning and development opportunities?

3. Who supports you and helps you to identify your customer service learning and development needs and activities?

4.6 Explain how to access sources of information and support for their learning

In the same way you research information about the products or services you offer to your customers, you should be prepared to research information and support for your own learning. It is important that you ask people in your organisation what is already available, for example your manager, team leader or supervisor. However, there are many other sources of information that you may find helpful:

- learning and development experts or personnel (human resource) departments
- suppliers and service partners
- manufacturers of products
- colleges, training providers and universities
- the internet – search engines such as Google and websites such as www. businessball.com
- company intranet (if available)
- public libraries
- manuals
- e-learning, distance learning.

Question

1. List at least four sources of support for your learning and explain how you can access each one.

4.7 Explain how to obtain useful and constructive personal feedback from others

Personal feedback is the feedback that relates to your performance, skills, knowledge, understanding and behaviour and can come from the following sources:

- your customers – compliments and complaints
- performance reviews and one-to-one meetings
- observation of your performance
- your manager, supervisor or team leader
- your colleagues.

There may be other sources of personal feedback available in your organisation. Often there are formal feedback systems in place and the feedback will emerge from self-assessment and reflection supported by managers, colleagues, suppliers, customers and others you come into contact within your role. This is known as 360-degree feedback because it comes from above and from others at the same level as you as well as others in the customer service chain. It can be very useful because it provides all-round feedback to help you to identify your strengths, areas for improvement and opportunities and threats.

Questions

1. Identify who could provide you with useful and constructive feedback on your performance.
2. What methods could you use to collect this feedback?
3. List the processes for gathering personal feedback that already exist in your organisation.

4.8 Describe how to respond positively to personal feedback

Many people find feedback difficult to handle, particularly if it can be seen as critical. However, as a customer service professional it is important to request constructive personal feedback from as many sources as possible. No one is perfect and the more you learn, the more you realise that learning never stops, especially with regard to human behaviour, technology and emerging products and services. No individual can stand still and although we can be inherently resistant to new products, systems and services, we must learn to live with change in the workplace. Feedback enables you to recognise successful behaviour or when a system or service has worked well and you can use this to build on those areas you need to improve. Instead of viewing feedback as a source of criticism, try to look at it as a 'gift' that enables you to improve your customer service.

In Tutorials 1 and 2 in Chapter 4 Unit A10, we looked at dealing with customers face to face and the behaviour and techniques that need to be applied to ensure it is a positive experience. Even if you do not regularly deal with your customers face to face it is important to use the same skills when a colleague, customer or manager provides you with feedback in person. Sometimes the way we perceive information is not the way the sender intended; your interpretation will depend on your feelings and emotions at the moment you receive the information. Look back and reflect upon the cycle of effective communication in Chapter 3 Unit A4 and at how the communication can fail on receipt.

Try the following tips for handling face-to-face feedback in a positive way.

- Create rapport: If you are face to face, try to relax and do not display defensive body language (such as folding your arms) because this can put the other person on the defence, particularly if they are conveying difficult feedback.

- Listen carefully: look for visual clues to support what the person is saying; sometimes facial expressions soften the words being spoken. Try not to interrupt the sender before they finish speaking.

- Process the information and then ask questions to clarify.

If the feedback is in a written format:

- Read the words carefully and process the content.

- Question the person who provided the feedback if there are phrases or words that you do not understand.

- Ask about the meaning and context of the feedback before jumping to conclusions.

Even if you do not agree with the feedback it is important to respond in an adult transactional state (see Tutorial 2, Chapter 3 Unit A4) and remain calm, logical and professional. If your questions do not bring the explanation you require then go away and think about the feedback and respond when you have prepared yourself. We tend to only focus on the areas we perceive as negative and these can overshadow the overall feedback. A reflective professional will underline or highlight the positives (either mentally or on paper) before considering the critical aspects. Feedback, viewed in a positive light, will enable you to analyse your performance to make improvements or build on your strengths.

Questions

Identify one example of positive feedback and one example of critical feedback that you have received about your personal customer service performance.

1. Describe each example – what was it and why was it given?

2. How did you react to the feedback and what did you do with it?

3. What were the differences in your reaction to the positive feedback compared with the critical feedback?

4. How can you prepare for and adapt your emotions to respond positively to constructive personal feedback?

Use your reflections to discuss this criterion with your assessor.

In Chapter 3 Unit A4 we looked at a case study about Liz who worked in a shoe shop. We will now revisit this case study to look at the situation from Liz's perspective and to examine what she has learned from the experience.

CASE STUDY 1 Liz's reflections

'I was working in the shop on Sunday 26 June. It was coming up to closing time and a customer came in and started looking at some of our sample shoes. The transaction did not go well and my manager, who was not in on the Sunday, received a letter of complaint from the customer the next day.

The customer said that I had made her feel stupid by my behaviour and attitude and her loyalty to our organisation had been damaged.

I was horrified and upset when my manager gave me this feedback. I became very defensive and he had to calm me down. We talked about the incident and we realised that I had been left alone quite a bit and I had only received training from the person who had left two days after I started. My manager said he must take some of the blame for my lack of knowledge of the procedures and legislation but I would need to reflect on my communication skills, my emotional behaviour and appearance. My manager did not get angry but he asked me to reflect on the incident and think about how I handled it and what I could change next time.

My manager gave me a reflective record and a SWOT analysis to complete. He said once I had completed these he would set up a development plan. He showed me a number of resources on our company intranet that I did not know existed and told me that the internet and the public library were good places to get information about legislation and regulations and communications skills.

I completed the SWOT analysis, reflected on this incident and I decided to take a look at the policies and information on our company intranet about sample shoes, refunds and exchanges. I realised that most of what I had told the customer was correct but that if the goods were faulty, and the fault was not because the shoes were damaged through incorrect use, then by law she could be entitled to a repair or a refund. I then went on to a government website and carried out more research. I also identified from this experience that the signs and leaflets that we have on display are not customer-friendly and we need to simplify the information and present it better.

At the next staff meeting I raised this incident and discussed it with the team and my manager. I offered to draft a display sign and leaflet about the policy for returns as I had already carried out the research on the internet. I also asked a few of our regular customers today whether they found the new sign and leaflet user friendly and clear. I made a few tweaks to the size of the wording and layout based on their feedback. The new information is now in place.

The other thing I raised at the meeting was the mistaken price because of the sticker left in the shoe. The team said this was not the first time it had happened and we agreed that we need to check every pair before we put them out on sale. I also offered to telephone the stockroom team supervisor at the warehouse and ask them to check that they have removed the price ticket before they send the shoes to us. I did this, and the supervisor was fine about it and I also sent an email to confirm what we agreed. He sent a note confirming the request and thanking me for highlighting the problem.

I know that I did not create a good rapport with the customer because I was hot, tired and was anxious to close the shop and get home. On reflection I feel bad about this. I will now make an effort not to let my personal feelings and emotions get in the way of work and also make sure that I look at my customer to read their body language and listen more closely to what they are saying. I have asked my manager if I can do a company online course on advanced communication skills to develop myself. He has put this on my development plan and I have already started it and had my first review.'

Questions

1. Complete the SWOT analysis form below on Liz's behalf (Figure D3.7). You will need to identify at least one point under each heading.

2. List three things that Liz has learned from this incident.

SWOT ANALYSIS

Strengths	Weaknesses

Opportunities	Threats

Figure D3.7: SWOT analysis for Liz

The reflective activity below is designed to help you to start thinking about your reactions and feelings when, as a customer, you have encountered different customer service scenarios. The activity will help you to prepare evidence that will demonstrate your knowledge, understanding and practical skills in customer service.

REFLECTIVE ACTIVITY

Collect your responses to the learner evaluation activity that appears at the end of each chapter in this book and use them as the foundation for a discussion with your assessor, see example below:

Performance evidence for Unit D3 (LO1, LO2 and LO3)

The tutorial questions, case study and reflective activity have given you the opportunity to identify your strengths and your areas for improvement as a customer service professional. So far you have looked at the importance of learning from your experiences and using the feedback that you receive, whether positive or negative, to improve your customer service.

The next section in this unit is designed to help you focus on the learning outcomes and performance requirement of Unit D3 and prompt you to think how you can evidence it through your customer service role.

Performance evidence is different from knowledge evidence and requires you to identify events that have happened in the course of your job in a real work environment. You will have to prove that the customers really exist and the events or incidents really happened – your assessor will help you to do this. The ways that you can present the evidence will be explained in Tutorials 2–5 below. You should answer the questions in the context of where you work and your provision of customer service. This time it *is* important for you to record your answers in writing as this will be the foundation of your evidence. However, you need only write notes to remind you where the proof is located.

LO1 Review performance in their customer service role

Assessment criteria
1.1 Work with an appropriate person to establish what they need to know, understand and be able to do to work effectively in their customer service role
1.3 Carry out a self assessment of their performance in their customer service role and identify their strengths, weaknesses and development needs

TUTORIAL 2 with your virtual advisor:

In order to evidence assessment criteria 1.1 and 1.3 you will need to identify the person within your organisation who can support you. Together you need to look at your job description or key performance indicators, work standards or service level agreement and assess:

- what you already know and understand
- what you can do
- where you need to improve.

Record the outcome on the SWOT analysis form on the next page or in the documentation supplied by your organisation.

During the process of working with your assessor they might be supporting you to identify areas for development and plan your customer service learning opportunities, through the use of a SWOT, learning styles questionnaire or an individual/personal learning plan. If this is the case, your assessor could act as your 'appropriate person' to meet the evidence requirements of this unit.

1.2 Identify and review situations from their own positive and negative experiences as a customer

If you have been undertaking the activities in the previous chapters you will have identified a number of situations that meet the requirements of assessment criterion 1.2; in addition, the reflective activity at the end of each chapter has required you to review both positive and negative experiences as the customer.

Reread the notes you made from your reflective activities and use these as a basis for a discussion or personal statement to cover this assessment criterion. Your assessor may be involved in helping you to identify these situations and you can discuss and reflect on the learning that has taken place. If this is the case, your assessor could act as your 'appropriate person' to meet the evidence requirements of this unit.

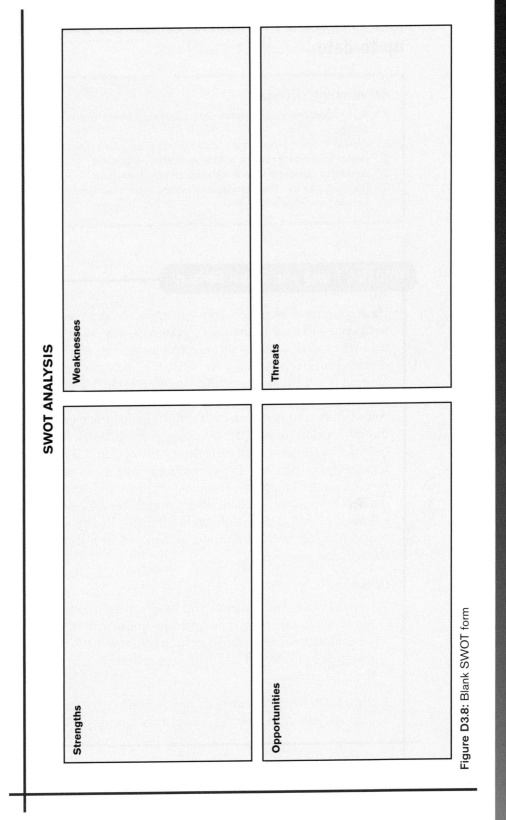

Figure D3.8: Blank SWOT form

LO2 Prepare a personal development plan and keep it up to date

Assessment criteria

2.1 Agree their strengths, weaknesses and development needs with an appropriate person

2.2 Work with an appropriate person to draw up their own development objectives to improve their performance in their customer service role

2.3 Develop a customer service personal development plan

2.4 Regularly review their progress towards their objectives with an appropriate person (see Tutorial 4 below)

TUTORIAL 3 with your virtual advisor:

Once you have identified your strengths, weaknesses and development needs you will need to draw up a plan of how to address them. There may be a set process within your organisation for this, referred to as a personal development review, a key performance indicator review, a one-to-one meeting or a performance quality audit or an annual appraisal. In the past these were seen as a one-way process, where your manager or supervisor told you whether your performance met the required standards and you accepted this information (or not). However, the personal development review should be a two-way process, with you taking equal responsibility with your manager for identifying what you do well and areas where you need to improve. The process should be about negotiating and agreeing how you can grow and develop in your role. It should bring mutual benefits to you, in the form of increased job satisfaction, skills and confidence, and your team, manager and organisation, in terms of having a professional well trained colleague, team member and employee.

Question

1. Use the notes and evidence you have collected for assessment criterion 4.5 earlier in this chapter and present an example of a SWOT exercise or a performance review carried out at work, together with the development plan that has emerged and been agreed with your appropriate person in the organisation.

If there is no procedure in place within your organisation then identify an appropriate person and use the exemplar documents provided in this chapter.

LO3 Undertake development activities and obtain feedback on their customer service performance

> **Assessment criteria**
>
> 3.1 Complete development activities identified in their customer service personal development plan
> 3.2 Use their day-to-day experiences with their customers and their own experiences as a customer to develop their customer service performance
> 3.3 Obtain feedback from an appropriate person about their customer service performance
> 3.4 Review and update their customer service personal development plan

TUTORIAL 4 with your virtual advisor:

If you return to the customer service professional's learning cycle at the beginning of this chapter you will see that your learning never stops. You will need to plan reviews with the appropriate person to assess how you have progressed with your learning. The content of the review will depend on you completing a journal or a reflective record. The reviews could be carried out at regular intervals or at the end of a learning activity, and the dates or review targets documented on the development plan.

Recording your experiences will come in useful as a tool to highlight the key stages of any type of learning undertaken, for example, a training course attended over a period of time, key incidents that have provided learning opportunities, research and reading. By recording your experiences you will be able to follow a structured evaluation of your learning journey and discuss with the appropriate person whether it has successfully contributed to your development as a customer service professional.

Questions

1. Using your organisation's documentation, reflect on at least two incidents or learning activities you have identified and undertaken recently. If you do not have documentation available within your organisation, use the reflective record in this chapter.

2. Use this information to review your learning with your appropriate person.

You have been asked to reflect on day-to-day activities in your customer service role and your experiences as a customer in every chapter of this book. By now you should have built up a bank of notes or personal statements from performance activities, reflective activities and tutorial questions that you can use to evidence assessment criterion 3.2. The information you have gathered will be helpful as a basis for a discussion with your assessor or to build a personal statement about your development activities. This will need to be supported by product evidence or witness statements.

It is possible that the evidence for learning outcomes 1 and 2 is naturally occurring in your organisation and you are already identifying your strengths, areas for improvement and development activities with a manager or supervisor. If this is the case, present the documentation or discuss the process with your assessor.

In addition to the learning outcomes in this unit, there are **evidence requirements** that indicate the circumstances or conditions under which you should present the evidence.

TUTORIAL 5 with your virtual advisor:

Evidence requirements provide the context in which you meet the assessment criteria for performance and enable your assessor to judge whether you are competent in a number of different situations. You do not need to cover the evidence requirements separately; they will be covered as you complete the assessment criteria. Your assessor will give you guidance. The evidence requirements for Unit D3 are explained below:

- An 'appropriate person' must be one or more of the following:
  - your manager
  - your supervisor or team leader
  - a colleague detailed to help you learn
  - your assessor
  - your mentor
  - someone from your training or personnel department.
- You will need to identify the appropriate person that you will be planning, discussing and agreeing your development needs with at the start of your evidence collection for this unit. If you find it difficult to locate an appropriate person in your organisation discuss this with your assessor and they might be able to discuss this with your manager or the training department.
- You must provide evidence that you have developed your personal development plan taking account of:
  - information about the knowledge and skills relevant to your customer service role
  - your own learning style preferences
  - your workload
  - opportunities for learning on the job.

We have considered the importance of constantly updating and developing the knowledge and skills relevant to your role. This should be embedded in your discussions with your appropriate person and link to the values and promises your organisation makes to their customers.

Earlier in this chapter we considered the importance of referring to different learning models in order to ascertain the best method of learning for your needs and circumstances. You may have been provided with a learning styles questionnaire at the start of your customer service qualification or when you have undertaken learning either within or outside your organisation. Use this information to help you gather your evidence of having selected development opportunities.

If you have not identified your learning style or completed a questionnaire or similar self-assessment, or it is not incorporated into the learning and development procedure in your organisation, go to www.businessballs.com for information regarding the VAK questionnaire or type 'learning styles' into a search engine to help you find a tool to identify your preferred learning style. Discuss the outcome with your manager, tutor or assessor.

- *Your personal development plan must be put on record and agreed with an appropriate person.*

It is vital that you have the support and agreement to progress your customer service learning and development from the appropriate person. If you have completed the activities in this chapter this will already have taken place and your appropriate person should have discussed, reviewed and endorsed the plan with you.

Evidence in context

An example of sample evidence for some of the learning outcomes of Unit D3 has been included at the end of the book.

Summary

This concludes the unit guidance for D3 Develop personal performance through delivering customer service.

You should be prepared to submit evidence for both the knowledge and performance aspects of the unit learning outcomes:

LO1: Review performance in their customer service role
LO2: Prepare a personal development plan and keep it up to date
LO3: Undertake development activities and obtain feedback on their customer service performance
LO4: Understand how to develop their personal performance through delivering customer service

You will now be able to describe how to reflect on your customer service role and events that occur in the course of your role and describe how you work in partnership with an appropriate person to identify your strengths and areas for improvement. You will be able to demonstrate how you produce and carry through development activities that have been recorded on a plan and agreed with an appropriate person.

It is likely that the knowledge and performance evidence you produce for the following units will cross-reference to this unit.

- Unit A10 Dealing with customers face to face
- Unit A11 Deal with incoming telephone calls from customers
- Unit B2 Deliver reliable customer service
- Unit C1 Recognise and deal with customer queries, requests and problems
- Unit D1 Develop customer relationships
- Unit F1 Communicate using customer service language
- Unit F2 Follow the rules to deliver customer service.

The evidence in this section has been presented as a guide to demonstrate how a personal statement or case study can cover and cross-reference to selected units within the qualification. Each of the examples provided are the learner's 'first draft' document where they have made suggestions about the assessment criteria that have been met in each unit. Their assessor will make the final judgement and provide feedback confirming if the evidence does indeed meet the requirements of the standards. This decision will be based on the statement and the supporting evidence the learner has submitted.

Sample assessment records

Mary Jones – Ivor Dent's problem pp 204–6
Liz Shoesmith – Sample shoe policy pp 207–9
May Smith – My call handling responsibilities pp 210–12

Candidate Name: Mary Jones   **Evidence Title:** Ivor Dent's problem

Qualification: Level 2 NVQ Certificate in Customer Service

Date: 12/8/11

(Please read the case study in Chapter 7 Unit C1 for the background to Ivor Dent's problem.)

I have identified the criteria that I think are covered in this case summary from:
Unit C1: AC 1.1, 1.2, 1.3, 1.4, 2.1, 2.2, 2.3, 2.4, 2.5, 2.6, 3.7
Unit D1: AC 1.1, 1.2, 2.1, 2.2, 2.3

My name is Mary Jones and I work on the customer service desk at Windruffs car showroom and dealers.

In May one of our regular customers, Ivor Dent, telephoned because he had had an accident – a car had gone into the back of him when he was waiting to come out of a side road. There was little external damage to his car but he wanted us to check it out for him to make sure that there was nothing wrong with the chassis. Mr Dent has recently purchased a new car from us so he was covered by a special service we have in place. We have an arrangement with B&S Insurance and we can offer a superior courtesy car while our customer's car is in for repair or checks. This is all organised by a colleague of mine, John Smith. My responsibility is to book the car in and email John to let him know when to come over to look at the car. I made the booking for Mr Dent and he came in at the allotted time a few days later. I called John and he came over and that was the last I heard about the situation. As far as I was aware it all went through with the insurance company.

A week ago, Mr Dent came in again. He said he had been booked in by my colleague, Reg, to put his car in for a courtesy check. I didn't take the booking as it was done when I was on holiday. However, I couldn't find the booking on our system. Reg is quite new and I have found that he is not very good at the paperwork and this isn't the first time things have gone wrong. I didn't say this to Mr Dent, as this would have been unprofessional. I could see from Mr Dent's body language and facial expressions that he was getting very agitated. I reassured him that I would sort the situation out. I asked him to take a seat and explained I was going to make a telephone call. I offered him a coffee and gave him the daily newspaper to read. I made a call to the service department (from the phone in the back office) and told them that a regular customer was booked in but the paperwork had not been processed. I have a good relationship with the manager over there so I asked him if he could fit in this job as I could see the customer was getting very unhappy. He asked me if I could hold on for a few minutes and then he would send someone over to collect the car. I went back to Mr Dent, who was still agitated and explained that the car would be taken over in about 10 minutes. I asked him if he had planned to stay at the showroom while the car was being serviced. He said that was what he had intended and he had some work to do. He explained he needed a plug socket as his laptop battery had run out of charge and he had a very important report to write and he needed a quiet area. I took him to our back office which was empty on that day. There are business facilities and free wireless connection to the internet. I wouldn't normally do this for a customer but I felt that on this occasion I needed to do a bit more than normal.

I took him to the office and I asked him if he was satisfied with the service that he had received from us so far. At this point he exploded and told me, in minute detail, about what had happened with the delivery of his courtesy vehicle when his car was in for repair in May. (See the case study in Chapter 7.) He told me he had given feedback on a number of occasions but nothing had come of it. He had told a number of people about the problem and they had thought it was terrible. The only reason he had come back to have the check today was because it was part of the aftercare package when he purchased the new car. He said today was the 'straw that broke the camel's back' and he had had it with Windruffs! Unit D1 AC 1.1, 1.2, 2.1, 2.2, 2.3

I remained calm. I empathised and tried to soften my verbal and body language. I said I was sorry that he was unhappy with the service he had received and the lack of response to his feedback. I made him comfortable in the office and provided all of the equipment and the code for the wireless network and explained that the car check would be about an hour, but that I would come and tell him when it was done. I explained that B&S Insurance was a separate organisation and I couldn't answer for their actions, although I could see that the incident has impacted on his satisfaction with Windruffs and the booking problem today hadn't helped. I said that while his car was being looked at I would investigate the problem and lack of response or apology to his feedback and see what I could do. Unit C1 AC 1.1, 1.4, 2.1, 2.2, 2.3, 2.4, 2.5, 2.6, 3.7

I went away and spoke to John Smith who had set the repair process up and Mike, another colleague, who had been given some feedback by Mr Jones. They said that it was really B&S Insurance's responsibility to sort it out and I was disappointed that they weren't willing to take some action. I said that if they gave me a contact number I would telephone B&S Insurance and speak to the relevant person, as I was concerned that this incident was having an adverse effect on Windruffs. I telephoned B&S Insurance and spoke to the supervisor of the team that had dealt with Ivor Dent's case. I explained what had happened and he was very puzzled about the error regarding the delivery address for the courtesy car but said he would investigate. In the meantime he said that he would arrange for some flowers to be delivered to Mr Jones as an apology. He also said he would contact Mr Jones and speak to him direct. Unit C1 AC 1.2, 1.3, 1.4

An hour later the car was ready so I returned to Mr Jones. He was in a much happier mood. He said that he didn't know what I had done but he had received a telephone call from Frank at B&S Insurance, apologising for the error. He had checked it up and there had been an inputting error which had never happened before. Frank had explained that Windruffs had done nothing wrong and that he would be receiving a gift and financial recompense for the loss of work, because Ivor had been unable to make his business meeting. He thanked me and said that under the circumstances he would stay with Windruffs. I assured him that I would follow up why he hadn't received any response to his feedback from us.

Yesterday I met with my manager and told him about the slip up that Reg had made and suggested that I take him through the process of booking paperwork again and I also told him about Mr Jones' problem. He said he would discuss the lack of response at the next managers' meeting and try to get some procedure in place so that this didn't happen again. He told me to arrange to send a 50% off car accessories voucher to Mr Jones, as a goodwill gesture. Today I received an email of thanks from Mr Jones. He (well, his wife) was delighted with the flowers that had arrived and pleased about the 50% off voucher, from Windruffs, as he was going to buy some wing mirror covers anyway. I was pleased with the outcome and have already started the training with Reg.

It just shows that a little extra 'TLC' and a bit of persistence can turn a bad situation around and you can retain your customer's loyalty.

Mary Jones

12/8/11

Supporting evidence:

Witness statement from John Smith, confirming I discussed the problem with him.

Thank you email from Mr Jones.

Notes that I made of the contacts at B&S Insurance.

Customer contact notes on the database in Mr Jones' file.

Statement from my manager about the follow-up meeting and actions.

Candidate Name: Liz Shoesmith **Evidence Title:** Sample shoe policy

Qualification: Level 2 NVQ Certificate in Customer Service

Date: 30/9/11

I have identified the criteria that I think are covered in this case study from:
Unit A4: AC 1.2, 1.3, 1.4, 1.5, 1.6, 1.7, 2.2, 2.4, 2.5, 3.2, 3.3
Unit D1: AC 3.1, 3.4, 3.5
Unit A10: AC 1.2, 1.3, 1.4, 1.6, 2.1, 2.2, 2.6
Unit D3: AC 3.1, 3.2, 3.3
Unit F2: AC 1.1, 1.2, 1.5, 2.1, 2.2, 2.6

In June I had an incident with a customer when I did not provide the service that I should have. I learned a few lessons about my rapport with the customer and at my own request I carried out some e-learning about communications. I also identified some issues about our refund policy signage and pricing information. I made some suggestions at a team meeting and by telephone and email with our service partners at the warehouse, to make improvements to the way we communicate our policies and procedures. Based on my experiences I now deal with customers with more sensitivity and understanding. Unit D1 AC 3.4 Unit D3: AC 3.1, 3.2, 3.3

I was working in the shop on Sunday 25th September and there were a number of customers in the shop. When they come in I always smile and say hello, good morning or good afternoon. I don't approach them straightaway but I observe them and look at their body language. Some are just looking, some try shoes on and some look at me as if they need some help. Today there was a customer who had been in earlier and then returned about an hour later. She was looking at a couple of pairs of our sample shoes we had displayed on the table in the middle of the shop. Both times the customer had come into the shop she tried them on. From my observation of her and her body language she seemed able to look after herself and she was wearing a pair of our brand of shoes, but last winter's style, so she was obviously a long-term customer. Unit A10 AC 2.1, 2.2, 2.6

This time I approached the customer and I made an opening comment about the shoes being this season's styles but on sale at a lower price because they are sample shoes. Unit A4 AC 1.2, 1.3, 2.2, 2.4. This started a conversation about the brand and the shoes she was looking at. I answered the questions about the price and her responses showed she was enthusiastic about the products. I needed to let her know about the policy for returns as this is different from the full price shoes, so I told the customer that sample shoes could not be returned if they didn't fit or she changed her mind about them, although she was still covered by her statutory rights under the Sale of Goods Act, which states that goods should be of suitable quality, fit for purpose and as described when sold. The customer asked me what this meant and I explained that the shoes should be of a good quality when sold to her, they should be fit for walking and general exercise but not for heavy rain or snow and ice and rugged terrain as there could be a danger of slipping, which is a health and safety risk. Unit A4 AC 1.4, 1.5, 1.6, 1.7, 2.5 We include a DVD about the shoes with every pair sold and this is important if the customer is new to our brand of shoe. I explained that the return policy for faulty goods will generally cover the customer if the shoe develops a fault (assumed to be present at purchase) up to six months after purchase. After this time it would be up to the customer to prove that the fault didn't occur through misuse of the product. The customer was very pleased with the information I supplied to her, but I did explain that there were a number of websites that provided information on a customer's statutory rights, so she could check if she wanted or needed to. Unit A4 AC 3.2, 3.3, Unit F2 AC 1.1, 1.2, 2.1, 2.2, 2.6

The customer asked me some more questions about availability of colours and I showed her all the stock in her size. I did tell her that the samples were only available in a limited range of styles but that we get them in once every three to four months. Unit D1 AC 3.1, 3.4, 3.5. Once they had been sold there would not be any more coming in for a while. I informed her that she could go onto our mailing list and we could let her know when the next batch of samples arrives. She thought that was a good idea. Unit A10 AC 1.2, 1.3, 1.4, 1.6. I left the customer to try the shoes again and to have a think about which ones she liked the best. I didn't hurry her even though it was closing time, but I locked the doors to stop any new customers coming in.

The customer made her decision and she came to the till. I provided her with one of our new leaflets about the returns policy. She asked if she could have a discount on the shoes (available to customers who live within the shopping complex), I explained that we only provided discount on full priced goods and the samples were already considerably less than the season's price. She said she realised the price was much less than normal and was happy with this explanation. She paid for the goods and I then asked her if she would like to take part in our customer feedback programme. We have been asked by head office (and given some training) to select some of our regular or long-term users to provide comments about the styles and durability of the shoes and the level of service they receive from our organisation. In return the customers receive a money voucher towards their next shoe purchase. The customer seemed pleased to be asked and said she was a big fan of our products. I took her email address and mobile telephone number so that we could send the questionnaires through to her. I informed her that the same details would set her up on our database for any sales and special offer information. I asked her what her preferred method of contact was. She said email and I asked her if she minded being contacted by text and she said that was fine as well. I reassured her that her details would be held on a secure system and they would not be passed to anyone outside our company (data protection compliant). Unit F2 AC 1.5.

I completed the sale by putting the shoes in a box which has a carrying handle so there is no need for a bag. I also explained about the care products that she should use on the shoes (we don't sell any in our shop) and where she could get them. The customer thanked me and I took the opportunity to ask her if she minded doing one final thing, which was to take a feedback card and write her comments down about today's experience which she could then drop back in the shop when she was next in. I explained that her name would be entered in our prize draw to win a pair of shoes up to the value of £120. She said that was fine as she would be back in the next couple of weeks to look at the winter boots that we had coming in.

As she left the store the customer thanked me and she made a comment to my manager about the service that she had received today. After she had gone he said that he would put her feedback into my one-to-one file along with any other feedback from customers and this would help at my performance and development review next week. I was much happier about the way I had dealt with this customer than the incident earlier in the year and I know that I have improved my body language, rapport and awareness of my customer's needs and feelings now. I also think it is great to be able to provide a customer with some additional information to help them understand our products and their rights and responsibilities. Unit D1 AC 3.4, 3.5

Supporting evidence:

- Updated leaflet about the sample returns policy

- Witness statement from my manager about the customer feedback and his observation of some of the customer transaction.

- My manager's confirmation that I entered the customer's details for the questionnaire and the promotion mailings.

- The database entry with the customer's details (not in the portfolio but can be seen on our system).

- My one-to-one file.

- The comments card from the customer

- Performance review.

- Development plan showing completion of communications e-learning.

I have already made some notes for a discussion for F2 learning outcome 2.

Liz Shoesmith

30/9/11

Candidate Name: Max Smith
Evidence Title: My call handling responsibilities

Qualification: Level 2 NVQ Certificate in Customer Service

Date: 2/9/11

I have identified the criteria that I think are covered in this personal statement from:

Unit F1: AC 1.1, 1.2, 1.3, 2.1, 3.1, 3.2, 3.6, 3.8
Unit F2: AC 1.1, 1.5, 2.5, 2.6,
Unit C1: AC 1.1, 2.1, 2.3, 2.4, 3.1, 3.5, 3.6,
Unit A11: AC 1.1
Unit D3: AC 1.1, 3.2, 4.1, 4.7

I work in the call centre (can be referred to as a contact centre) for the police in the county of Westchester. I am responsible for handling telephone calls, emails, fax and text communications from members of the public, councils, social services and also neighbouring police services and specialist crime services within the criminal justice system. I also have customers calling from abroad. All of these people are my external customers.

I am also responsible for dealing with communications to and from police officers, police community support officers and police staff within the Westchester Constabulary – these are my internal customers. My service partners are the force control room (where all the emergency calls are taken), the staff on the front desks in the police stations and specialist services like CID, forensics and child protection. Although they are my internal customers at times we collaborate on cases when required. I also handle some emergency calls when the force control room is busy.

Unit F1: AC 1.1, 2.1, 3.1, 3.2

I have a role profile detailing what I am expected to do in my job, which is linked to the competencies in my learning and development review document. (See my role profile.)

I never know what types of calls I will receive until I start talking to my callers. My customers are all ages, from young children through to vulnerable adults. They might not speak English as their first language and they could have some type of physical impairment, for example, be hard of hearing. I have to be prepared to adapt my communication style to the needs and expectations of each customer. (See example in my quality checks.)

F1 AC 3.8

The purpose of the call to us might be because there has been a theft, a report about noisy neighbours, a request for information about aspects of the law as well as emergencies such as a traffic accident or a threat to someone's life.

Because we are a police call centre we often receive calls from customers who are distressed and often angry and abusive. I have to know how to react and be sensitive to their needs, but I also have to know when I cannot help them until they calm down. I have to be really careful and make an accurate assessment of the risks they may be under. I cannot take any chances so I often speak to my supervisor for advice before I make a final decision. I have to be prepared for anything which is why I have a training period of one year. About 15 weeks was spent in the class room working alongside a tutor, but since then my call handling and customer service has been closely monitored by my tutor through listening to my calls. In addition my supervisor checks all my record keeping each time I have to write up a call on our bespoke database. I get regular feedback from day-to-day activities if I need to improve my skills or if I didn't meet all of the assessment criteria when I answered the call. (I have included some examples of both positive and developmental feedback in the links.)

Unit C1 AC 1.1, 2.1, 2.3, 2.4, 3.1, 3.5, 3.6

I work with a variety of equipment, including a telephone and computer. I must have an awareness of different types of software, word processing and spreadsheets and emails, also telephone systems and databases tailored for the organisation. We have an opening up routine when we have to clean the phone, computer and desk with bacterial wipes and make sure the desk is the right height for my comfort and safety. Then I log on to the system with passwords and security checks. I always have to agree I will comply with Data protection regulations on log-in. I have been observed by my tutor carrying out all the activities and my competence has been assessed and documented in the quality checks. My supervisor has listened in to my calls on a number of occasions. (See examples.)

Unit A11 AC 1.1

Many people within the police can access this record system so my inputting and communications have to be accurate, complete and legally correct. A mistake could cost a life if I filed a record under a non-emergency code, as this might result in a police officer not considering the call a priority. There is a policing charter (see example) on the internet endorsed by our Chief Constable and everything we do in terms of customer service links back to that. I have service standards, a response time for answering calls, making the greeting and other key points of the call (this is called the shape of the call). I am assessed formally against these standards and given feedback at least once every two months. I see these sessions as very helpful, although I used to get a bit nervous, as my manager gives me constructive feedback and wants me to improve. These sessions are recorded on a document she keeps on the system in a secure area and she emails me a copy so I can see how I am progressing. She also sends me complimentary comments and emails from internal and external customers and tells me to store them so that I can use them when I have to write my self assessment for my progress review (every four months at the moment).

F1 AC 3.6

I need to be aware of legal and regulatory requirements relating to human rights, data protection, disability discrimination, health and safety, criminal law and local council regulations. We have a site on our intranet where criminal law and any legislation information is regularly updated. If there have been any patterns of crimes in an area or there are issues or changes to procedures then this information will be updated. We have to read this page at the start of every shift in case of any updates. There are also other websites that we can access for information and a who's who of contacts and subject specialists. This is very useful if I cannot answer a customer's question or query.

My team is made up of twelve people and we work shifts. We also work alongside another team and some of our shifts overlap. We have a good team and we can discuss problems or issues about procedures together. We also discuss types of calls so that we can standardise our approach and what we say to the customers. Once every month we have a team meeting and the supervisors will let us know the team targets and our results for the month and this is where we will also discuss changes to systems and any issues we have about policies and procedures. We are encouraged to put forward our ideas for improvement based on front-line experiences. One of my ideas has already been considered: this was about recording information more accurately, and I received a letter of commendation from the Chief Inspector (CI). I will provide details of this in a personal statement supported by the minutes of our meeting and the letter from the CI. There are about six teams that cover the call centre and we have mini competitions to see which team is performing the best. Our targets are also linked to government targets. I will provide some examples of the feedback I have received, my progress reviews and call monitoring as supporting evidence to this statement.

Unit F1 AC 1.2, 1.3

Unit F2 AC 1.1, 1.5, 2.5, 2.6

I will provide some examples of calls and emails about lost property, nuisance, crime and emergencies that I have dealt with later in my portfolio. I think there might be other areas of the qualification covered in this report and supporting evidence.

Supporting evidence:

- Screen print of the policing charter on the internet and our customer promises
- My role profile (job description) and linked competencies
- My objectives linked to the customer promise
- Review documentation (learning and development review)
- Letters and emails, compliments
- Quality checks and live audit results from my supervisor and tutor
- Minutes of the team meeting showing my contribution
- List of contacts and the intranet briefing page (can be seen on the computer)

Max Smith

2/9/11

GLOSSARY

Added value an additional benefit in terms of usefulness or convenience
something extra, over and above the standard product or service

Analyse to examine in detail in order to discover meaning, essential features, etc.

Apply to devote oneself with diligence
to bring into operation or use
to put to practical use; utilise; employ

Assess to judge the worth or importance of; evaluate

Behaviour the way that you do things
the way in which a person or group responds to a specific set of conditions

Benefit something that has a good effect or promotes wellbeing

Body language (non-verbal) bodily mannerisms, postures and facial expressions that can be interpreted as unconsciously communicating somebody's feelings or psychological state

Carry out to perform or cause to be implemented

Classify to arrange or order by classes; categorise

Collect to gather together or be gathered together

Communicate to impart (knowledge) or exchange (thoughts, feelings or ideas) by speech, writing, gestures

Compare to regard or represent as analogous or similar; liken

Competitor an organisation that offers products or services that are similar to those offered by your organisation

Compile to make or compose from other materials or sources

Complete to make whole or perfect to end; finish

Conduct to do or carry out

Constructive carefully considered and meant to be helpful

Contract an agreement between two parties that can be enforced by law

Contrast to distinguish by comparison of unlike or opposite qualities

Contribute to give (support, money, etc.) for a common purpose or fund
to supply (ideas, opinions, etc.) as part of a debate or discussion

Customer a person or company that buys goods or services
somebody who interacts with others in a particular way
a person or organisation to whom goods or services are provided and sold
a user of the services offered by another organisation

Customer Charter a statement of what an organisation will do for their customer

Customer feedback feedback is information about customer perceptions of customer service collected by the organisation from customers or given to the organisation by customers

Customer service the sum total of what an organisation does to meet customer expectations and produce customer satisfaction

Define to state precisely the meaning of (words, terms, etc.)

Deliver to carry (goods, etc.) to a destination; to carry and distribute (goods, mail, etc.) to several places

to hand over, transfer or surrender
to produce or perform something promised or expected

Demonstrate to show, manifest or prove, especially by reasoning, evidence, etc.

Describe to give an account or representation of in words

Design to work out the structure or form of (something)

Detail to list or relate fully
to include all or most particulars

Develop to come or bring to a later or more advanced or expanded stage; grow or cause to grow gradually

Development an incident that causes a situation to change or progress

Devise to work out, contrive or plan (something) in one's mind

Discuss to have a conversation about; consider by talking over; debate
to treat (a subject) in speech or writing

Emotional intelligence Understanding of feelings, personal attributes that enable people to succeed in life, including self-awareness, empathy, self-confidence and self-control

Evaluate to ascertain or set the amount or value of
to judge or assess the worth of; appraise

Examine to look at, inspect or scrutinise carefully or in detail; investigate

Explain to make (something) comprehensible, especially by giving a clear and detailed account of the relevant structure, operation, surrounding circumstances, etc.

Explore to examine or investigate, especially systematically

Expectations a confident belief or strong hope that a particular event, service or product will meet the needs of an individual

External customer a person or company that buys goods or services somebody who interacts with others in a particular way a person or organisation to whom goods or services are provided and sold a user of the services offered by another organisation a private individual or from another organisation

Features a part of something that distinguishes it

Generate to produce or bring into being; create

Give to present or deliver voluntarily (something that is one's own) to the permanent possession of another or others to impart or communicate

Identify to prove or recognise as being a certain person or thing; determine the identity of

Illustrate to clarify or explain by use of examples, analogy, etc.

Implement to carry out; put into action; perform

Interact to act on or in close relation with each other

Internal customer somebody from the same organisation as the service provider a user of the services offered within the same organisation a customer from another part of the same organisation

Interpret to clarify or explain the meaning of; elucidate

Investigate to inquire into (a situation or problem) thoroughly; examine systematically, especially in order to discover the truth

Justify to prove or see to be just or valid; vindicate

to show to be reasonable; warrant or substantiate

Keep to have or retain possession of

Lead to show the way to (an individual or a group) by going with or ahead to guide or be guided by holding, pulling, etc. to phrase a question to (a witness) that tends to suggest the desired answer

Legislation a law or laws passed by an official body

Limitations an imposed restriction that cannot be exceeded or sidestepped a legal restriction on the powers that somebody has

Loyalty (customer) a feeling of attachment to an organisation or product

Mentor an experienced professional who advises and guides a less experienced member of staff

Mission statement a brief statement of the main purpose or objectives of the organisation

Moments of truth the points in a transaction, service delivery or customer relationship at which customer expectations are at their sharpest and most demanding

Monitor to observe or record (the activity or performance) of (an engine or other device)

Mystery shopper/consumer a tool used by organisations to measure the quality of products or services and compliance to legislation regulation.

Objectives an aim or goal

Organise to form (parts or elements of something) into a structured whole; coordinate

Outline to give the main features or general idea of

Participate to take part, be or become actively involved or share (in)

Perform to carry out or do (an action)

Plan to have in mind as a purpose to make a plan of (a building)

Practice an established way of doing something, especially one that has developed through experience and knowledge

Prepare to make ready or suitable in advance for a particular purpose or for some use, event, etc. to put together using parts or ingredients; compose or construct to equip or outfit

Present to show, exhibit to put forward; submit to bring or suggest to the mind

Problem (customer service) a question or issue that needs to be solved when the customer service does not meet customer expectations

Procedure an established or correct method of doing something

Produce to bring (something) into existence; yield to bring forth (a product) by physical or mental effort; make

Promote to further or encourage the progress or existence of to raise to a higher rank, status, degree, etc. to urge the adoption of; work for to encourage the sale of (a product) by advertising or securing financial support

Propose to put forward (a plan, motion, etc.) for consideration or action

Provide to put at the disposal of; furnish or supply

Recognise to perceive (a person, creature or thing) to be the same as or belong to the same class as something previously seen or known; know again

Recommend to advise as the best course or choice; counsel

Reflect to think seriously, carefully and relatively calmly

Regulation an official rule, law or order stating what may or may not be done or how something must be done

an order issued by a government department or agency that has the force of law

Relationship the connection between two or more people or groups and their involvement with one another, especially as regards the way they behave towards and feel about one another

Research to carry out investigations into (a subject, problem, etc.)

Resources Source of help, money, people, supplies or equipment

Review to look at or examine again

to look back upon

Select to choose (someone or something) in preference to another or others

Serve to render or be of service to (a person, cause, etc.); help

to distribute or provide

Service offer the extent and limits of the customer service that an organisation is offering

Service partnership two organisations or two departments of the same organisation combine in order to provide more effective customer service

Service provider an organisation that provides customer service

Show to make, be or become visible or noticeable

to indicate or explain; prove

Suggest to put forward (a plan, idea, etc.) for consideration

Summarise to make or be a summary of; express concisely

Timeliness occurring at a good time; happening or done at the right time or an appropriate time

Transaction an instance of doing business of some kind, e.g. a purchase made in a shop or a withdrawal of funds from a bank account

a communication or activity between two or more people that influences and affects all of them

Transactional analysis (TA) a framework for describing behaviour in an interchange between two people

Understand to know and comprehend the nature or meaning of

Undertake to contract to or commit oneself to (something) or to do (something)

Use to put into service or action; employ for a given purpose

Variation to the service offer offering something that differs slightly from the norm

INDEX

Note: Numbers in **bold** indicate a glossary entry.